COOKING FOR FUN

GREAT IDEAS FOR CASUAL ENTERTAINING

COOKING FOR FUN

GREAT IDEAS FOR CASUAL ENTERTAINING

Anne Ager

CONTENTS

ANOTHER BEST-SELLING VOLUME FROM HPBooks®

Publisher: Rick Bailey; Editorial Director: Retha M. Davis; Editor: Jeanette P. Egan; Art Director: Don Burton
Book Assembly: Leslie Sinclair; Typography: Cindy Coatsworth, Michelle Claridge
Book Manufacture: Anthony B. Narducci
Recipe testing by International Cookbook Services: Barbara Bloch, President; Rita Barrett, Director of Testing

Notice: The information contained in this book is true and complete to the best of our knowledge. All recommendations are made without any guarantees on the part of the author or HPBooks. The author and publisher disclaim all liability in connection with the use of this information.

Published by HPBooks, Inc.
P.O. Box 5367, Tucson, AZ 85703   602/888-2150
ISBN 0-89586-341-3
Library of Congress Catalog Card Number 85-60087
© 1985 HPBooks, Inc. Printed in the U.S.A.
1st Printing

Originally published as The Fun Food Book © 1983 Hennerwood Publications Limited
Cover Photo: Orange-Cup Trifles, page 77; Salami & Pita Specials, page 44.

Introduction

Eating is necessary, but it doesn't have to be boring! Essentially, food should be fun—fun to prepare, and fun to eat. Many children may start to cook by playing with pastry or cookie dough. Their products often end up limp and grey. No matter, if children are involved in food preparation at an early age, their interest in food and cooking grows.

Too often food preparation is left to one member of the household, but cooking can be a family affair. Children, husbands and even guests can get involved in meal preparation. The idea of this book is to add a little extra sparkle and imagination to everyday eating by involving other members of the family and guests when possible. Although some of the recipes are out of the ordinary, all of them are geared to family eating and entertaining. They are imaginative without being difficult.

THE GREAT OUTDOORS

This chapter includes food ideas for family picnics and barbecues in the backyard. There are many appropriate foods to choose from. Picnics can be elegant or casual, but picnic foods need to be sturdy and easily transported. There is a wide range of special equipment for keeping foods hot or cold, such as ice chests and vacuum bottles. These may be worth the investment if you picnic a lot. Remember that fresh air tends to increase appetites; make sure that you provide generous quantities of everything.

TABLE-TOP COOKING

Whether for family eating or entertaining, cooking at the table is great fun. Guests enjoy cooking or preparing food for themselves when being entertained, hence the popularity of the fondue. A fondue-type meal can be a perfect choice for a family occasion, too. For meat fondues cooked in oil, use a metal fondue pot that is not easily tipped. Cheese and chocolate fondues need to be protected against scorching. Use pottery or ceramic fondue pots and a low flame. Other top-of-the-table cookware include electric skillets, chafing dishes or attractive skillets with an adjustable burner underneath. Most of the preparation, chopping and slicing are done in the kitchen. Sometimes the actual cooking is done in the kitchen; then the cooked dish is kept warm over a burner or in a chafing dish over hot water. However, doing the actual cooking at the table is an excellent way to impress guests. And, it's fun for guests to cook for themselves.

FOOD ON A SKEWER

Food on a skewer is another novel way of presenting a meal for family or friends. Many foods, such as good-quality steak, chicken and seafood, cook quickly. When these are cut into small pieces and threaded on skewers, they cook quickly on the outside but are still succulent and moist in the center. Fruit kabobs make appetizing dishes and are a change from the more traditional main-dish kabobs.

Skewers come in a variety of sizes, but an 11-inch skewer is the one most commonly used. This is the size skewer that has been used in most of the recipes in this book. Small metal and bamboo skewers are available. If using bamboo skewers, soak in water 30 minutes before using to prevent the bamboo from scorching during cooking.

Do not pack food tightly when threading it on a skewer. Otherwise, it will cause the food to cook unevenly and affect cooking time. Foods on the skewer should touch, but not be pressed together.

Kabobs can be cooked under a broiler or over an outside barbecue grill. Remember to preheat grill or broiler before using. The distance the food is from the source of heat determines the speed at which it will cook. Ideally, a kabob should cook about 4 inches away from the heat source; this ensures thorough cooking, without the food becoming charred. If your broiler is much higher than this, then raise the food on a baking pan or something of a convenient size that is heatproof. Alternatively, you can cook kabobs on a barbecue. Remember that food usually cooks faster on a barbecue. Reduce the cooking time slightly, and watch the food carefully to prevent burning. Use special wood chips or mesquite charcoal to add interesting flavors to barbecued foods.

SPECIAL SANDWICHES

Sandwiches come in many different forms, from the simple two-layered variety with a mere filling to multi-layered sandwiches, laden with a variety of ingredients. This chapter provides a selection of special sandwiches. There are ideas for cocktail sandwiches, toasted sandwiches, party sandwiches and those suitable for family suppers.

When making sandwiches, vary filling and bread to give interesting combinations. Or for a sandwich party, provide a variety of fillings, condiments and breads; let everyone create their own favorites.

Toaster ovens have become increasingly popular. They are excellent for preparing a quick, hot snack. The last five recipes in this chapter are for toasted sandwiches, using a conventional broiler. Sandwiches can also be toasted in a toaster oven or on a grill. Follow the manufacturer's instructions when using special equipment for cooking sandwiches.

ALL WRAPPED UP

Wrapping food in pastry, foil, paper or other wrappings

before cooking adds an interesting touch. There is nothing new about cooking in packages. People have been cooking food in foil since it was first introduced. In the Middle East, food has been wrapped in leaves before cooking for thousands of years. In Latin America, banana leaves are often used for cooking. However, you can be original in choosing the wrapping and in choosing the food to be wrapped. There are a few *en croute* recipes using short crust and puff pastries. Or, bake spaghetti in a parchment-paper bag. Leaves are not neglected either; recipes are included for foods wrapped in spinach and cabbage leaves.

FAMILY TREATS

This chapter contains unusual and colorful food ideas for the whole family. Some would make ideal presents to give at Christmas or other special occasions. If there is some supervision from an adult, many of the recipes are simple enough for children to make for themselves.

Clockwise from bottom left: Pear Dumpling, Peanut Sandwich Balls, Banana Pops

The Great Outdoors

Barbecue Bites

Juice of 2 lemons
1/4 teaspoon ground ginger
Salt
Freshly ground pepper
2 firm avocados, halved, peeled
18 bacon slices

These small bacon and avocado bundles make a perfect appetizer while everyone is waiting impatiently for steaks or hamburgers to grill.

1. Preheat grill. In a medium bowl, combine lemon juice, ginger, salt and pepper. Cut each avocado half into 9 equal pieces. It does not matter if they are not all quite the same shape. Toss avocado cubes in the lemon-juice mixture.
2. Cut each bacon slice in half crosswise. Roll up each cube of avocado in a piece of bacon. Thread on 6 small skewers.
3. Place on preheated grill. Cook 2 to 3 minutes or until bacon is crisp. Makes 6 servings.

Barbecued Spareribs

4 lb. pork spareribs
Marinade:
6 tablespoons soy sauce
1/4 cup vegetable oil
3 garlic cloves, crushed
1 teaspoon grated gingerroot or 1/4 teaspoon
   ground ginger
Grated peel of 1 lemon
Few drops of hot-pepper sauce
1/2 teaspoon ground cinnamon
Salt
Freshly ground pepper
1/4 cup honey

There is not much meat on spareribs. If they are to be served as a main course, allow about one pound per person. To cook spareribs more quickly, separate into individual ribs.

1. Preheat grill. Cut spareribs into individual ribs, if desired.
2. To make marinade, in a small bowl, combine all ingredients except honey.
3. Place spareribs on preheated grill, bone-side down; brush with marinade. Cook about 10 minutes. Turn ribs over; brush with more marinade. Cook 15 minutes more.
4. Turn ribs again; brush with marinade and honey. Cook 10 to 15 minutes more or until ribs are tender. Makes 4 main-dish servings.

Arabian Orange Salad

4 oranges, peeled
1 medium onion, cut into thin rings
1/4 cup sliced black olives

Dressing:
6 tablespoons olive oil
Juice of 1/2 lemon
1 tablespoon chopped fresh mint
1 tablespoon chopped pine nuts or blanched almonds
1 tablespoon chopped raisins
Salt
Freshly ground pepper

1. Remove white bitter pith from oranges. Cut into thin slices, discarding any seeds. Arrange orange slices, onion and olives in a shallow dish.
2. To make dressing, in a small bowl, combine oil, lemon juice, mint, nuts, raisins, salt and pepper. Spoon evenly over orange mixture. Cover; refrigerate 1 hour for flavors to blend.
3. To take on a picnic, pack salad in a tightly covered container. Makes 4 servings.

Top to bottom: Barbecued Spareribs, Barbecue Bites, Arabian Orange Salad

Left to right: Chicken Salad Paprika with Pasta, Cheese & Watercress Flan

Chicken Salad Paprika with Pasta

3 lb. cooked chicken
1 cup mayonnaise
1/2 cup dairy sour cream
1 tablespoon paprika
2 tablespoons tomato paste
1/2 teaspoon sugar
4 large tomatoes, skinned, seeded, chopped
Salt
Freshly ground pepper
Pasta
6 oz. pasta wheels or shells
1 small onion, finely chopped
About 6 tablespoons oil-and-vinegar dressing
2 tablespoons chopped fresh parsley

1. Cut chicken into small cubes, discarding skin and bones.
2. In a medium bowl, combine mayonnaise, sour cream, paprika, tomato paste, sugar and tomatoes. Season with salt and pepper. Stir in chicken cubes until coated. Cover; refrigerate 2 to 3 hours.
3. To make Pasta, cook pasta according to package directions until tender but firm. Drain cooked pasta thoroughly.
4. While pasta is still warm, in a large bowl, combine drained pasta, onion and enough oil-and-vinegar dressing to moisten. Set aside until cool. Stir in chopped parsley and additional dressing, if necessary.
5. To take on a picnic, pack chicken salad and pasta in separate containers. Keep chilled. Serve chicken salad over pasta. Makes 4 to 6 servings.

Variation
If desired, add 3 chopped hard-cooked eggs to chicken salad. If too thick, add 1 or 2 tablespoons milk.

Cheese & Watercress Flan

Pastry for a 9-inch pie crust
1 (8-oz.) pkg. cream cheese, room temperature
1/2 cup dairy sour cream
2 eggs, separated
Salt
Freshly ground pepper
1 (1/4-oz.) envelope unflavored gelatin (1 tablespoon)
1/4 cup chicken stock or water
1 bunch watercress (about 2 oz.), washed, shaken dry
1/4 cup finely chopped green onions

1. Preheat oven to 400F (205C). On a lightly floured surface, roll out pastry to an 11-inch circle. Use pastry to line a 9-inch quiche pan or flan pan with removable bottom. Line dough with foil; fill with pie weights or dried beans.
2. Bake in preheated oven 10 minutes. Remove foil and pie weights; bake 5 minutes more. Cool on a wire rack.
3. In a medium bowl, beat cream cheese, sour cream, egg yolks, salt and pepper until blended. Set aside.
4. In a small saucepan, combine gelatin and chicken stock or water. Stir well; let stand 3 minutes. Stir over low heat until gelatin dissolves; set aside to cool. Stir into cheese mixture; set aside.
5. Remove coarse stems and any discolored leaves from watercress; finely chop. In a medium bowl, beat egg whites until stiff but not dry. Set aside 2 tablespoons chopped watercress for garnish. Fold beaten egg whites, remaining chopped watercress and onions into cheese mixture. Spoon mixture into cooled pastry shell; smooth top.
6. Refrigerate 2 to 3 hours or until set. Sprinkle top of flan with reserved chopped watercress.
7. To take on a picnic, leave flan in pan. Wrap with plastic wrap or foil; keep chilled. Makes 4 to 6 servings.

Swedish Meat Patties

3 white-bread slices, crusts removed
1/2 cup club soda
8 oz. ground veal
8 oz. ground pork
2 oz. ham, finely chopped
1 teaspoon juniper berries, crushed
2 egg yolks
Salt
Freshly ground pepper
Vegetable oil

To serve:
4 large rye-bread slices, spread with unsalted butter
1 medium onion, cut into thin rings
2 dill pickles, cut into wedges
2 tablespoons capers
1/2 cup dairy sour cream

1. Break bread into small pieces. In a small bowl, combine bread pieces and club soda. Let stand 20 minutes.
2. Preheat grill. In a medium bowl, combine veal, pork, ham, juniper berries and egg yolks. Season with salt and pepper. Stir in bread mixture until smooth. Form into 4 flat patties. Refrigerate 30 minutes.
3. Brush patties with oil. Place on preheated grill. Cook 4 minutes. Turn patties; brush with oil. Cook 4 minutes more or until juices are no longer pink.
4. Place a rye-bread slice on each serving plate. Place a grilled patty on each slice. Garnish with a few onion rings, dill pickles and a small spoonful of capers. Add a dollop of sour cream to each plate. Makes 4 servings.

Scandinavians are masters at making meatballs and meat patties. They combine a variety of ground meats with subtle seasonings, such as juniper berries, dill seed and ground allspice. One secret is the addition of club soda to the basic mixture to lighten the texture. Meatballs are often served slightly rare or pink. If pork is used in the meat mixture, cook until well-done. Bread slices are used to absorb the delicious meat juices.

Maple Chicken

4 chicken legs
Marinade:
2/3 cup unsweetened orange juice
1 medium onion, thinly sliced
1 garlic clove, crushed
Salt
Freshly ground pepper
Freshly grated nutmeg
1/4 cup maple syrup

Maple syrup gives chicken a pronounced maple flavor. If desired, substitute a mild honey. The flavor is enhanced by marinating overnight.

1. Pierce chicken legs at regular intervals with a fine skewer. Place pierced chicken in a shallow dish. Add orange juice, sliced onion and garlic. Season with salt, pepper and nutmeg. Cover; refrigerate 8 hours or overnight.
2. Preheat grill.
3. Remove chicken from marinade, allowing excess to drip off. Place on preheated grill; cook 15 minutes. Turn over; brush with maple syrup. Cook 15 to 20 minutes or until chicken is tender. Test chicken by piercing in thickest part with a small skewer. If juices run clear, chicken is done. Serve hot. Makes 4 servings.

Orange & Watercress Salad

4 oranges
1 bunch watercress, washed, shaken dry
1 small onion, finely chopped
1/4 cup olive oil
2 tablespoons chopped fresh chives or parsley
Salt
Freshly ground pepper

---

1. Grate peel and squeeze juice from 1 orange. Peel remaining oranges with a small sharp knife. Section peeled oranges.
2. Cut watercress into sprigs. Place orange sections and watercress sprigs into a shallow serving dish; sprinkle with onion. In a small bowl, combine orange juice, orange peel, olive oil and chives or parsley. Season with salt and pepper. Spoon dressing over salad. Makes 4 servings.

Top to bottom: Swedish Meat Patties, Maple Chicken with Orange & Watercress Salad

Cheesy Meat Loaf

3/4 lb. lean ground beef
3/4 lb. lean ground pork
2-1/2 cups fresh bread crumbs
1 egg, beaten
1/2 cup beer
1 teaspoon dried rosemary, crushed
Salt
Freshly ground pepper
1 small onion, finely chopped
1 cup diced Edam cheese

To garnish:
Radish halves
Green onions
Watercress

This meat loaf is cooked on a rack rather than in a loaf pan to allow the fat from the pork to drain off during cooking. Since this meat loaf is served cold, it is important to remove the fat.

1. Preheat oven to 350F (175C). In a medium bowl, combine beef and pork until blended.
2. Place bread crumbs in another medium bowl. Stir in egg, beer, rosemary, salt and pepper. Pour over meat; stir in bread-crumb mixture, onion and cheese.
3. Shape mixture into loaf; smooth top. Place on a rack in a baking pan.
4. Bake in preheated oven 1-1/2 hours.
5. Discard fat. Cool meat loaf to room temperature. When cool, wrap in plastic wrap or foil; refrigerate until thoroughly chilled.
6. To take on a picnic, unwrap. Slice meat loaf; rewrap. Keep chilled until ready to serve. When ready to serve, arrange on a serving plate; garnish with radishes, green onions and watercress. Makes 6 servings.

Tomato Vichyssoise

3 tablespoons butter or margarine
1 medium onion, finely chopped
2 cups peeled, coarsely chopped potatoes
2 cups coarsely chopped tomatoes
1 garlic clove, crushed
1 tablespoon tomato paste
1 tablespoon chopped fresh basil or 1 teaspoon
    dried leaf basil
1-1/2 cups chicken stock
1-1/2 cups milk
Salt
Freshly ground pepper
1/2 cup whipping cream

To garnish:
Chopped fresh parsley or basil

This soup makes a delicious starter for a barbecue meal. Or, pack chilled soup in a thermos to take on a picnic.

1. Melt butter or margarine in a medium saucepan. Add onion; sauté 3 minutes. Add potatoes, tomatoes, garlic, tomato paste, basil, stock and milk. Season with salt and pepper. Bring to a boil; simmer 25 to 30 minutes or until potatoes are tender.
2. Press soup through a sieve. Or, process soup in a blender or food processor fitted with a steel blade until smooth. Cool pureed soup; stir in cream.
3. Refrigerate until chilled. Garnish with chopped parsley or basil. Serve with crusty bread, if desired. Makes 6 servings.

Left to right: Cheesy Meat Loaf, Strawberry-Cheese Mousse

Strawberry-Cheese Mousse

1 (15-oz.) container whole-milk ricotta cheese (2 cups)
1/2 cup sugar
1 teaspoon vanilla extract
2 eggs, separated
1/2 pint whipping cream (1 cup)
1 (1/4-oz.) envelope unflavored gelatin (1 tablespoon)
1/4 cup water
1 pint strawberries, washed, hulled

To decorate:
Sweetened whipped cream, if desired

1. Lightly oil an 8-inch heart-shaped pan.
2. In a medium bowl, beat ricotta cheese, sugar, vanilla, egg yolks and cream until smooth and blended.
3. In a small saucepan, combine gelatin and water. Stir well; let stand 3 minutes. Stir over low heat until gelatin dissolves; set aside to cool. Beat into cheese mixture. Refrigerate until mixture mounds when dropped from a spoon.
4. Set 8 large strawberries aside for decoration. Coarsely chop remaining strawberries.
5. In a medium bowl, beat egg whites until stiff but not dry. Fold beaten egg whites and chopped strawberries into cheese mixture. Pour mixture into oiled pan; refrigerate 3 to 4 hours or until set.
6. Unmold on a flat serving plate. Decorate with reserved strawberries and whipped cream, if desired. Makes 6 to 8 servings.

Potted Blue Cheese

3 cups crumbled Stilton cheese or other
  blue cheese (12 oz.)
1/2 cup unsalted butter, room temperature
Freshly ground pepper
Pinch of grated nutmeg
3 tablespoons port
2 tablespoons chopped blanched almonds, toasted
Few whole toasted almonds

1. In a medium bowl, blend cheese and butter.
2. Season with pepper and nutmeg. Beat in port and chopped almonds.
3. Press cheese mixture into a small crock or other serving dish. Top with whole almonds.
4. Refrigerate to store. Bring to room temperature before serving. Makes about 3 cups.

Brown-Sugar & Chestnut Meringues

3 egg whites
3/4 cup firmly packed light-brown sugar
1/2 cup whipping cream
1/4 cup sweetened chestnut puree

1. Preheat oven to 250F (120C). Grease 2 baking sheets; line with parchment paper.
2. In a medium bowl, beat egg whites until soft peaks form. Add 1/2 of sugar; beat until stiff and glossy. Fold in remaining sugar.
3. Spoon mixture into a pastry bag fitted with a large star tip. Pipe 20 large meringue rosettes on prepared baking sheets.
4. Bake in preheated oven 2 hours or until dry. Cool completely on baking sheets on wire racks. Peel off parchment paper.
5. In a small bowl, whip cream until stiff peaks form. Fold in chestnut puree.
6. Spread chestnut cream over bottoms of 1/2 of meringues. Sandwich together with remaining meringues. Makes 10 meringues.

Clockwise from top left: Rich Cherry & Almond Dessert, No-Bake Nut Cake, Brown-Sugar & Chestnut Meringues

Rich Cherry & Almond Dessert

1 (16-oz.) can pitted dark sweet cherries
6 eggs, separated
1/2 teaspoon almond extract
3/4 cup sugar
1 cup all-purpose flour
2 tablespoons unsweetened cocoa powder
3 tablespoons butter or margarine, melted
1/4 cup red-currant jelly
6 oz. semisweet chocolate, melted
1/4 cup sliced almonds

This cake has a very moist texture. If making this cake for a special occasion, sprinkle 3 to 4 tablespoons of brandy over the cake instead of cherry syrup and melted jelly.

1. Preheat oven to 350F (175C). Grease a 10-inch spring-form pan; line with waxed paper.
2. Drain cherries, reserving 6 tablespoons syrup. Pat cherries dry with paper towels; set aside.
3. In a large bowl, beat egg yolks and almond extract until thickened and lemon-colored. In a medium bowl, beat egg whites until soft peaks form. Gradually beat in sugar; beat until stiff and glossy.
4. Fold beaten egg-white mixture into egg-yolk mixture. Sift flour and cocoa over mixture; fold in. Fold in butter or margarine.
5. Spoon half of batter into prepared pan; smooth top.
6. Bake in preheated oven 10 minutes. Remove from oven; arrange cherries over baked layer. Pour remaining batter over cherries; smooth top. Bake 40 to 45 minutes more or until center springs back when lightly pressed. Cool in pan on a wire rack 15 minutes.
7. Carefully remove cake from pan; peel off paper. Place cake, right-side up, on a wire rack set over a jelly-roll pan.
8. Place reserved cherry syrup and jelly in a small saucepan. Stir over low heat until jelly is melted. Prick top of cake with a skewer. Spoon jelly mixture over cake. Let stand until cake is completely cool. Spread melted chocolate over top of cake and around side. Lightly press almonds around side and top edge of cake. Wrap cake well to keep moist. Makes 10 to 12 servings.

Variation

Substitute canned pear pieces, thin pineapple chunks or mandarin oranges for cherries. Make sure that all canned fruit is drained thoroughly before using. The red-currant, chocolate and almond topping is suitable with most fruits.

No-Bake Nut Cake

1/2 (16-oz.) box graham crackers (16 whole crackers), coarsely crumbled
3/4 cup chopped mixed candied fruit
1 cup red candied cherries, chopped
3/4 cup raisins
1 cup chopped nuts
1 teaspoon pumpkin-pie spice
2 cups marshmallows
3 tablespoons sweet sherry
3 tablespoons molasses
4 oz. semisweet chocolate, broken into small pieces

1. Lightly grease a 9" x 5" loaf pan. Line pan with waxed paper; grease paper.
2. In a medium bowl, combine cracker crumbs, candied fruit, candied cherries, raisins, nuts and spice. Set aside.
3. Place marshmallows, sherry, molasses and chocolate in top of a double boiler over simmering water. Stir until mixture is melted and smooth. Stir chocolate mixture into cracker mixture until blended.
4. Spoon mixture into prepared pan; smooth top. Cover with greased waxed paper. Refrigerate 4 hours or until cake is firm.
5. Invert pan on a serving plate. Remove pan; peel off waxed paper. Cut into 12 to 14 slices. Makes about 12 servings.

Steaks with Green-Peppercorn Sauce

2 tablespoons butter or margarine
2 tablespoons vegetable oil
4 (1/2-inch-thick) beef top loin or tenderloin steaks
1/2 cup whipping cream
1 garlic clove, crushed
2 teaspoons green peppercorns
Salt
1 tablespoon chopped fresh parsley

1. Heat butter or margarine and oil in an electric skillet or decorative skillet over an adjustable burner.
2. Add steaks; sauté 2 minutes on each side for medium-done or to desired doneness.
3. With tongs, place steaks on a plate; keep warm.
4. Stir cream, garlic, green peppercorns, salt and parsley into fat remaining in skillet.
5. Cook 1 minute; return steaks to skillet. Cook 1 minute. Makes 4 servings.

Fondue Bourguignonne

1-1/4 lb. beef-loin tenderloin

To garnish:
Parsley sprigs, watercress or lettuce
Vegetable oil for deep-frying

To serve:
Accompanying sauces, see opposite
French bread
Green salad

1. Cut tenderloin into 1/2-inch cubes. Arrange on 4 individual plates, garnishing meat with parsley, watercress or lettuce.
2. Fill a metal fondue pot 1/2 full of oil. Heat oil to 375F (190C) or until a 1-inch bread cube turns golden brown in 50 seconds.
3. Provide each person with a plate of cubed meat, a fondue fork for spearing and cooking meat, and a knife and fork for eating.
4. Each person cooks his or her own steak in hot oil to desired doneness.
5. Provide a selection of dipping sauces, a basket of hot French bread and a green salad. Makes 4 servings.

Sauces for Fondue Bourguignonne

Horseradish Sauce

1 tablespoon prepared horseradish
Juice of 1/2 lemon
Pinch of sugar
1/2 cup dairy sour cream
Salt and pepper

In a small bowl, combine all ingredients. Makes about 1/2 cup.

Mustard Sauce

1 small onion, finely chopped
1/2 cup mayonnaise
1 tablespoon prepared brown mustard
1/2 teaspoon red (cayenne) pepper
Salt

In a small bowl, combine all ingredients. Makes about 1/2 cup.

Green Sauce

2 tablespoons capers
4 gherkins
2 garlic cloves
1/4 cup olive oil
1/4 cup white-wine vinegar
2 tablespoons coarsely chopped fresh parsley
Pinch of sugar
Salt and pepper

In a blender or food processor fitted with a steel blade, process all ingredients until smooth. Makes about 1/2 cup.

Cold Curry Sauce

1/2 cup whipping cream, whipped
1 tablespoon mild curry powder
Finely grated peel of 1/2 lemon
1 tablespoon raisins
Salt

In a small bowl, combine all ingredients. Makes about 1 cup.

Clockwise from top: Steaks with Green-Peppercorn Sauce, Fondue Bourguignonne with Cold Curry Sauce, Green Sauce and Mustard Sauce

Seafood & White-Wine Fondue

1 (12-oz.) white-fish fillet
3/4 cup all-purpose flour
1/2 teaspoon baking powder
Salt
1 egg
1/2 cup water
Vegetable oil for deep-frying

Fondue:
5 tablespoons butter or margarine
1/2 cup all-purpose flour
1 cup chicken stock
1-1/2 cups dry white wine
Salt
Freshly ground pepper
1/2 cup whipping cream
3 egg yolks

To dip:
6 oz. deveined, peeled, cooked shrimp
8 oz. shelled cooked mussels

1. Cut fish fillet into 1-inch squares.
2. Sift flour, baking powder and salt into a medium bowl. Add egg and 1/2 of water; beat until smooth. Beat in remaining water.
3. Fill a deep pan 1/3 full of oil. Heat to 375F (190C), or until a 1-inch bread cube turns golden brown in 50 seconds. Dip fish pieces into batter. Carefully add coated fish to hot oil; fry 3 minutes or until crisp and golden. Drain on paper towels.
4. If prepared in advance, heat fried fish in a 375F (190C) oven to crisp.
5. To make fondue, melt butter in a medium saucepan; stir in flour. Cook 1 minute constantly.
6. Gradually stir in chicken stock and wine until sauce is smooth and thickened. Season with salt and pepper.
7. Transfer wine mixture to a fondue pot or chafing dish; place over a low flame.
8. In a small bowl, beat cream and egg yolks. Gradually stir cream mixture into hot wine mixture. Do not allow to boil.
9. Divide crispy fish pieces, shrimp and mussels among 4 individual plates.
10. To eat, dip fish, shrimp and mussels into hot fondue. Accompany with chunks of hot French bread. Makes 4 servings.

Beer & Gouda Fondue

1 garlic clove, crushed
1 cup dark beer
3-1/2 cups shredded Gouda cheese (14 oz.)
1 tablespoon all-purpose flour
Freshly ground pepper
1 teaspoon caraway seeds

To dip:
1 French-bread loaf, cut into 1-inch cubes

Left to right: Beer & Gouda Fondue with French bread, Seafood & White-Wine Fondue

This fondue is quite thick. Do not use too high a heat when melting cheese.

1. Rub inside a fondue pot with garlic; discard garlic.
2. Pour beer into seasoned fondue pot. Heat over low heat until beer starts to boil.
3. In a medium bowl, combine cheese and flour. Stir cheese mixture into hot beer until smooth.
4. Season with pepper. Stir in caraway seeds.
5. Keep warm over a low flame. Serve with bread cubes. Makes 4 servings.

Cottage-Cheese & Chive Fondue

8 oz. dry cottage cheese (1 cup)
1 cup shredded Swiss cheese (8 oz.)
1-1/2 tablespoons all-purpose flour
1 cup white wine or unsweetened apple juice
1 tablespoon Worcestershire sauce
2 teaspoons prepared brown mustard
2 tablespoons chopped fresh chives
Salt
Freshly ground pepper

To dip:
1 French-bread loaf, cut into 1-inch cubes

1. Press cottage cheese through a sieve. In a medium bowl, combine sieved cottage cheese, Swiss cheese and flour.
2. Pour wine or juice into fondue pot. Heat until wine or juice starts to boil.
3. Stir cheese mixture into hot wine or juice until smooth.
4. Stir in Worcestershire sauce, mustard and chives. Season with salt and pepper.
5. Keep warm over a low flame. Serve with bread cubes. Makes 4 servings.

Crab Fondue

1 garlic clove, crushed
1 cup dry white wine
2-1/2 cups shredded mild Cheddar cheese (10 oz.)
1 tablespoon all-purpose flour
Salt
Freshly ground pepper
6 oz. white crabmeat, flaked

To dip:
Puff-pastry crescents or cheese straws

1. Rub inside a fondue pot with garlic; discard garlic.
2. Pour white wine into seasoned fondue pot. Heat until wine starts to boil.
3. In a medium bowl, combine cheese and flour. Stir cheese mixture into hot wine until smooth.
4. Season with salt and pepper. Stir in crabmeat.
5. Keep warm over a low flame. Serve with crescents or cheese straws. Makes 4 servings.

Chinese Fondue

1 qt. chicken stock (4 cups)
1 onion, thinly sliced
1 large carrot, sliced
1 celery stalk, chopped
4 large mushrooms, sliced
3 thin slices fresh gingerroot

To dip:
6 oz. tiny button mushrooms
1 small Chinese cabbage, shredded
1/2 small cauliflower, divided into flowerets
4 oz. Chinese pea pods or 2 cups small spinach leaves
4 oz. peeled, deveined, uncooked shrimp
6 oz. boneless chicken, cut into thin strips
6 oz. calves' liver, cut into thin strips
6 oz. beef-loin tenderloin, cut into thin strips
6 oz. pork-loin tenderloin, cut into thin strips

To serve:
Cooked rice or noodles
Accompanying sauces, see below

1. In a medium saucepan, combine stock, onion, carrot, celery, mushrooms and ginger. Simmer 10 minutes.
2. Arrange mushrooms, cabbage, cauliflower, pea pods or spinach, shrimp, chicken, liver, beef and pork decoratively on a platter.
3. Transfer stock mixture to a Chinese hot-pot or fondue pot; place over a burner.
4. When stock is hot, each person cooks his or her own food. After all cooking is finished, serve the flavored stock in soup bowls or cups. Serve with hot cooked rice or noodles and a choice of sauces. Makes 4 to 6 servings.

Chinese Sauces

Soy & Garlic Sauce

1/2 cup soy sauce
3 garlic cloves, crushed

In a small saucepan, simmer soy sauce and garlic 1 to 2 minutes. Serve warm or cool. Makes 1/2 cup.

Plum Sauce

6 tablespoons plum jam
2 tablespoons vinegar
2 tablespoons chopped mango chutney

In a small bowl, combine all ingredients. Serve at room temperature. Makes 1/2 cup.

6 tablespoons olive oil
3 green onions, finely chopped
1 garlic clove, crushed
1 tablespoon sesame seeds
Salt and pepper

In a small bowl, combine all ingredients. Makes about 1/3 cup.

Lime & Pepper Sauce

Juice of 2 limes
Salt and pepper
1 red pepper, finely chopped
1 small onion, finely chopped
3 tablespoons olive oil

In a small bowl, combine all ingredients. Makes about 1/3 cup.

Tomato Sauce

1/4 cup tomato sauce
1/2 teaspoon chili powder
2 teaspoons soy sauce
1 garlic clove, crushed
Salt
1 teaspoon sugar
Juice of 1 lemon

In a small bowl, combine all ingredients. Makes about 1/2 cup.

Almost a complete chapter could be written on this classic Chinese-style fondue. It is usually referred to as a *Mongolian hot-pot* or *fire-pot*. Well-flavored stock is substituted for hot oil for cooking.

An attractive array of foods is presented alongside the hot-pot. All foods are cut into small pieces for quick cooking. Foods often cooked this way include whole peeled shrimp; thin strips of chicken, pork, veal, liver, or lean tender beef; small button mushrooms or soaked dried mushrooms; Chinese cabbage strips; cauliflowerets; spinach leaves and Chinese pea pods.

For a richer flavor, add sliced onion, green-pepper strips, carrot slices, chopped celery or mushroom slices to the stock at the beginning of cooking. Add fresh gingerroot, if desired. The flavor of the stock will improve as the meal progresses. If you do not have the special Chinese hot-pot, substitute an attractive saucepan or fondue pot with a burner. Each person uses chopsticks or a small wire ladle for cooking food in the hot stock. Forks can be used for eating, if desired. Soup bowls and soup spoons will be needed for eating the flavored stock after the meat, fish and vegetables have been eaten.

Accompany the hot-pot with bowls of hot rice or noodles and two or more well-flavored sauces for dipping. Five sauce recipes are included.

Top tray: Clockwise from top left: Tomato Sauce, Green-Onion Sauce, Plum Sauce, Lime & Pepper Sauce

Top to bottom: Chinese Fondue, Foods prepared for cooking, Cooked noodles

Spring Rolls

12 egg-roll skins, thawed, if frozen
Filling:
3/4 cup finely chopped cooked chicken
1 tablespoon soy sauce
4 Chinese cabbage leaves, coarsely shredded
3 green onions, coarsely chopped
4 water chestnuts, finely chopped
Freshly ground pepper
1 egg white

Sweet & Sour Sauce:
2 tablespoons cornstarch
1 cup chicken stock
1/4 cup red-wine vinegar
1/4 cup packed brown sugar
1 tablespoon tomato paste
2 teaspoons soy sauce
Vegetable oil for deep-frying

Chinese spring rolls are a perfect choice for cooking at the table.

1. Remove egg-roll skins from package. Cover with a damp cloth to prevent drying.
2. To make filling, in a medium bowl, combine chicken, soy sauce, cabbage, onions and water chestnuts. Season with pepper.
3. To fill spring rolls, spoon 1 to 2 tablespoons filling on bottom corner of 1 egg-roll skin. Fold lower corner of skin over filling; roll once. Brush side corners with egg white; fold both sides in toward center. Roll again. Brush upper corner of skin with egg white. Roll into a tight package. Repeat with remaining skins and filling. Place spring rolls on waxed paper; cover with a towel until ready to deep-fry. These can be refrigerated overnight, if desired.
4. To make sauce, in a small saucepan, combine cornstarch and 1/4 cup stock. Stir in remaining stock, vinegar, sugar, tomato paste and soy sauce; bring to a boil. Stir until sauce is smooth and thickened.
5. Fill a metal fondue pot 1/3 full of oil; heat to 375F (190C) or until a 1-inch bread cube turns golden brown in 50 seconds.
6. Carefully place spring rolls into hot oil; deep-fry 2 to 3 minutes on each side or until crisp and golden.
7. Drain spring rolls on paper towels. Serve hot with sauce. Makes 6 servings.

> Do not overcook fish. It is already tender and cooks quickly. Cook only until firm and opaque. To test for doneness, cut into the center of the thickest part. It should be slightly opaque. One rule is to cook fresh fish 10 minutes per inch of thickness and to cook frozen fish 20 minutes per inch of thickness. However, this is only a general guide; cooking time will vary with the oven temperature and the shape and type of fish. Overcooked fish is tough and dry.

Clockwise from bottom left: Unrolled Spring Rolls, Fried Spring Rolls, Pan-Fried Trout with Grapes

Pan-Fried Trout with Grapes

4 trout, filleted
1/4 cup butter or margarine
1 small onion, finely chopped
Grated peel of 1/2 lemon
6 tablespoons dry white vermouth
2 tablespoons chopped fresh parsley
Salt
Freshly ground pepper
1/4 cup whipping cream
4 oz. seedless green grapes

1. Remove any bones from trout.
2. Melt butter or margarine in an electric skillet or decorative skillet over an adjustable burner.
3. Add trout, skin-side up; sauté 2 to 3 minutes. Turn trout; sauté 2 to 3 minutes more.
4. With a spatula, place trout on a heated plate.
5. Add onion, lemon peel, vermouth and parsley to skillet. Boil until mixture is reduced by half. Season with salt and pepper.
6. Stir in cream; return trout to skillet. Add grapes; cook 1 minute. Do not boil.
7. Serve immediately. Makes 4 servings.

Veal Escalopes with Sage

4 veal cutlets, thin sliced, pounded
2 tablespoons butter or margarine
2 tablespoons vegetable oil
1 small onion, finely chopped
1 tablespoon chopped fresh sage or
    1 teaspoon rubbed sage
2 oz. ham, cut into strips
1-1/4 cups sliced mushrooms (3 oz.)
Salt
Freshly ground pepper
3 tablespoons brandy
1/4 cup whipping cream

To garnish:
Fresh sage leaves, if desired

---

1. Cut veal into 2-inch squares.
2. Heat butter or margarine and oil in an electric skillet or decorative skillet over an adjustable burner. Add onion; sauté until onion is softened.
3. Add veal squares; sauté 1 to 2 minutes per side or until tender. With tongs, place sautéed veal on a plate; keep warm.
4. Add sage, ham and mushrooms to fat remaining in skillet; sauté 2 minutes.
5. Season with salt and pepper. Stir in brandy and cream; bring almost to a boil.
6. Return sautéed veal to skillet; heat in sauce 1 minute.
7. Garnish with fresh sage leaves, if desired. Makes 4 servings.

Spiced Lamb Sauté

1-1/4 lb. lamb leg
1/4 cup butter or margarine
1 medium onion, finely chopped
1 garlic clove, crushed
1/2 teaspoon ground cinnamon
2 teaspoons cornstarch
1/2 cup chicken stock
1/2 cup dairy sour cream
1 tablespoon chopped fresh mint
Salt
Freshly ground pepper

---

1. Cut lamb into thin slices about 1/4-inch thick.
2. Melt butter or margarine in an electric skillet or in a decorative skillet over an adjustable burner.
3. Add onion, garlic and cinnamon; sauté until onion softens.
4. Add slices of lamb; sauté, turning occasionally, until lamb is browned on all sides.
5. In a small bowl, blend cornstarch, stock and sour cream. Stir cornstarch mixture into lamb mixture.
6. Stir until sauce thickens slightly. Add mint; season with salt and pepper. Simmer 8 to 10 minutes or until lamb is tender.
7. Serve hot with noodles or rice. Makes 4 servings.

Veal with Spicy Tomato Sauce

1-1/2 lb. veal cutlets
Lettuce leaves
Vegetable oil for deep-frying

Spicy Tomato Sauce:
1/2 cup dairy sour cream
3 tablespoons tomato paste
1 tablespoon Worcestershire sauce
1 tablespoon prepared brown mustard
1 garlic clove, crushed
Salt
Freshly ground pepper

---

1. Cut veal cutlets into 2" x 1/4" strips. Line 4 small individual plates with lettuce. Arrange veal strips over lettuce.
2. Add enough oil to fill fondue pot 1/2 full. Heat oil to 375F (190C) or until a 1-inch bread cube turns golden in 40 seconds.
3. To make sauce, in a small bowl, combine all ingredients.
4. Each person cooks veal in hot oil 20 to 30 seconds. Serve with sauce, hot crusty bread and a green salad. Makes 4 servings.

Top to bottom: Veal Escalopes with Sage, Spiced Lamb Sauté

Flambéed Bananas

1/4 cup butter or margarine
4 large bananas, peeled
1/4 cup dark rum
2 tablespoons brown sugar

To serve:
Wedges of lime or lemon
Whipped cream

1. Melt butter or margarine in an electric skillet or decorative skillet over an adjustable burner.
2. Cut bananas in half lengthwise.
3. Add bananas to hot butter or margarine; sauté 1 minute, turning bananas in butter or margarine.
4. Pour rum over bananas. When warm, carefully ignite rum.
5. When flames die down, sprinkle bananas with brown sugar. Baste with butter-and-rum sauce.
6. Serve hot with wedges of lime or lemon and whipped cream. Makes 4 servings.

Peanutty Chocolate Fondue

1 (6-oz) pkg. peanut butter flavored pieces
1 (6-oz) pkg. milk chocolate pieces
1 (14-oz.) can sweetened condensed milk
1/2 cup milk

To dip:
Banana slices
Marshmallows
Pound-cake or sponge-cake cubes

1. In a medium saucepan, combine all ingredients for fondue. Stir over low heat until peanut butter pieces and chocolate pieces are melted and mixture is smooth.
2. Pour into a fondue pot or chafing dish. Keep warm over low heat.
3. Serve with banana slices, marshmallows and cake cubes. Makes 4 to 6 servings.

Cherry Compote

2 (15-oz.) cans dark sweet cherries
1/4 cup packed brown sugar
Finely grated peel of 1/2 orange
1/4 cup kirsch

To serve:
Vanilla ice cream

1. Drain cherries, reserving 2/3 cup syrup.
2. Place reserved syrup in an electric skillet or in a decorative skillet over an adjustable burner; heat.
3. Stir in sugar and orange peel until sugar dissolves. Cook over low heat until syrup has reduced slightly.
4. Add cherries to hot syrup; heat through.
5. Heat kirsch in a small saucepan. When warm, carefully ignite kirsch; pour over cherries.
6. When flame dies down, serve hot with ice cream. Makes 6 servings.

Chocolate & Honey Fondue

1 cup milk
1-1/2 tablespoons cornstarch
1/2 pint half and half (1 cup)
6 oz. semisweet chocolate, grated
1/4 cup honey
Finely grated peel of 1/2 orange

To dip:
Pound-cake or sponge-cake cubes
Crystallized-ginger pieces
Marshmallows

1. In a medium saucepan, blend 1/4 cup milk and cornstarch until smooth.
2. Stir in remaining milk, half and half, chocolate, honey and orange peel.
3. Stir milk mixture over low heat until chocolate melts.
4. Cook until fondue thickens, stirring constantly.
5. Pour into a fondue pot or chafing dish. Keep warm over low heat.
6. Serve with cake cubes, ginger pieces and marshmallows. Makes 4 to 6 servings.

Lemon Fondue

1 pint whipping cream (2 cups)
5 egg yolks
Finely grated peel of 3 lemons
5 tablespoons sugar

To dip:
Gingerbread cubes

1. Heat cream in top of a double boiler over simmering water until warm. Or, use a heatproof bowl over a pan of simmering water.
2. In a medium bowl, beat egg yolks, lemon peel and sugar until thick and creamy.
3. Beat warm cream into egg-yolk mixture.
4. Return lemon mixture to top of double boiler; cook until fondue mixture coats back of a spoon, stirring frequently.
5. Spoon fondue into a chafing dish or heatproof bowl; place over simmering water.
6. Serve with gingerbread cubes. Makes 4 to 6 servings.

Left to right: Flambéed Bananas, Chocolate & Honey Fondue with cake, crystallized ginger and marshmallows for dipping

Pineapple with Caramel Sauce

1 small fresh pineapple
6 tablespoons kirsch or brandy
6 tablespoons butter or margarine
3 tablespoons brown sugar
Grated peel and juice of 1 small orange

To serve:
Whipping cream

Substitute rings of canned pineapple for fresh pineapple, if desired. However, the flavor will not be quite as good.

1. Remove pineapple top and peel. Remove eyes with a sharp-pointed knife or vegetable peeler.
2. Cut pineapple into 8 equal slices.
3. Put pineapple slices into a shallow dish; spoon over 1/4 cup of kirsch or brandy. Cover; refrigerate 3 to 4 hours.
4. Drain chilled pineapple slices, reserving liquid.
5. Melt butter in an electric skillet or decorative skillet over an adjustable burner.
6. Stir in brown sugar; cook until mixture bubbles. Stir in orange peel and juice.
7. Add slices of pineapple to caramel sauce; cook 2 minutes. Add reserved liquid from pineapple.
8. In a small saucepan, heat remaining kirsch or brandy. When warm, carefully ignite kirsch or brandy. Pour flaming kirsch or brandy over pineapple.
9. When flame dies down, serve pineapple with whipping cream. Makes 4 servings.

Left to right: Pineapple with Caramel Sauce, Mocha Fondue with marshmallows and bananas for dipping

Mocha Fondue

1 pint whipping cream (2 cups)
3 tablespoons freshly ground coffee or
  2 tablespoons instant coffee powder
5 egg yolks
5 tablespoons sugar

To dip:
Banana chunks
Marshmallows

Two tablespoons instant coffee can be used for this fondue, but ground coffee gives it a much better flavor. This fondue contains eggs and will curdle. To prevent curdling, do not use too hot a temperature. The best way to avoid curdling is to pour the fondue into a chafing dish or heatproof bowl. Then to serve, place chafing dish or bowl over a pan of simmering water. If using a bowl, make sure that bowl will not tip.

1. In a medium saucepan, heat cream until warm.
2. If using ground coffee, add to warm cream. Cover; steep in a cool place 3 to 4 hours. Strain cream. If using instant coffee powder, follow instructions for ground coffee; do not strain.
3. Heat coffee-flavored cream in top of a double boiler over hot water.
4. In a medium bowl, beat egg yolks and sugar. Beat egg-yolk mixture into hot coffee-flavored cream.
5. Cook until mixture will coat back of a spoon.
6. Transfer mixture to a heatproof bowl or chafing dish; place over simmering water.
7. Serve with banana and marshmallows. Makes 6 servings.

When making fondue for young children, the safest way to serve it is to ladle the hot fondue into small warmed soup bowls. This gives each child his or her own portion. There is no danger of tipping over a hot fondue pot. Give each child a small plate with some of the banana, marshmallows or other accompaniments.

Food on a Skewer

Middle-Eastern-Style Kabobs

1 medium eggplant
Salt
8 small white onions
2 medium zucchini, cut into rings 1/2 inch thick
1 red bell pepper, cut into cubes
8 cherry tomatoes
1/2 cup plain yogurt
1 garlic clove, crushed
1/2 teaspoon ground ginger
3 tablespoons olive oil
Salt
Freshly ground black pepper

To serve:
Mozzarella-cheese or feta-cheese slices
Olive oil

These kabobs are rather crunchy. If you prefer vegetables that are more tender, blanch them before grilling.

1. Cut eggplant roughly into 1-inch cubes. Place eggplant cubes in a colander; sprinkle with salt. Let stand 30 minutes.
2. Simmer onions in boiling water 5 minutes. Drain onions.
3. Rinse eggplant cubes; pat dry with paper towels.
4. Thread rinsed eggplant, cooked onions, zucchini, bell pepper and tomatoes on 4 kabob skewers.
5. In a small bowl, combine yogurt, garlic, ginger, olive oil, salt and pepper.
6. Place kabobs in a large shallow dish. Spoon yogurt mixture over kabobs. Cover and refrigerate 3 hours.
7. Preheat broiler or grill. Gently shake kabobs to remove excess yogurt mixture.
8. Broil kabobs about 4 minutes on each side, brushing with a little yogurt mixture.
9. Sprinkle mozzarella-cheese or feta-cheese slices with olive oil. Serve with hot kabobs. Makes 4 servings.

Mixed Fruit Kabobs

Coconut Cream:
3 tablespoons shredded coconut
1/4 cup boiling water
1/2 cup whipping cream, thickly whipped

Kabobs:
1/2 cup fresh orange juice
Juice of 2 lemons
5 tablespoons sugar
1 pear, peeled, cut into 8 pieces
2 small firm bananas, peeled, cut into 4 pieces
2 fresh or canned pineapple slices, cut into 8 pieces
8 pitted cherries or seedless grapes
4 small preserved stem-ginger pieces
2 tablespoons warm honey
Brown sugar
2 tablespoons flaked almonds

This could be called fruit salad on a stick! Children will love it. It is equally suitable for an informal dinner party.

1. To make Coconut Cream, in a small bowl, combine coconut and boiling water. Let stand 30 minutes. Strain through a sieve, pressing coconut to extract flavor and liquid. Whisk coconut milk into thickly whipped cream. This can be prepared ahead.
2. In a medium bowl, combine orange juice, lemon juice and sugar.
3. Stir in pear, bananas, pineapple, cherries or grapes, and preserved ginger until evenly coated in juice mixture. The juice prevents fruit discoloration.
4. Preheat broiler. Drain fruit thoroughly; thread alternately on 4 kabob skewers.
5. Put fruit kabobs on a broiler-pan rack. Brush with honey; sprinkle with brown sugar and almonds.
6. Broil 3 to 4 minutes or until kabobs are light golden.
7. Serve immediately with Coconut Cream. Makes 4 servings.

Top to bottom: Middle-Eastern-Style Kabobs, Mixed Fruit Kabobs with Coconut Cream

Top to bottom: Chicken-Liver & Water-Chestnut Kabobs,
Apple-Sausage Kabobs

Apple-Sausage Kabobs

1/4 cup dry bread crumbs
1/4 teaspoon rubbed sage
1 teaspoon dried onion flakes
1/2 cup boiling water
1 lb. bulk pork sausage
1 egg yolk
Salt
Freshly ground pepper
2 red-skinned apples, cut into wedges
Juice of 1 lemon
Vegetable oil

1. In a medium bowl, combine bread crumbs, sage, onion flakes and water. Let stand until water has been absorbed.
2. Stir in sausage and egg yolk. Season with salt and pepper.
3. Shape into small balls about the size of a walnut; refrigerate 1 hour.
4. In a medium bowl, toss apple wedges in lemon juice.
5. Preheat broiler. Thread sausage balls and apple wedges alternately on 4 kabob skewers.
6. Place kabobs on a broiler-pan rack. Brush with oil. Broil 5 minutes. Turn; brush with oil. Broil 5 to 6 minutes or to desired doneness. Makes 4 servings.

Chicken-Liver & Water-Chestnut Kabobs

1 lb. chicken livers, rinsed, dried
8 bacon slices
8 water chestnuts, halved
2 tablespoons soy sauce
1/4 cup vegetable oil
Freshly ground pepper

Bacon slices will roll easily if you stretch them slightly on a flat surface.

1. Cut chicken livers into 16 equal pieces.
2. Cut bacon slices in half crosswise.
3. Roll up 1 piece of chicken liver and 1 water chestnut half in a half-slice of bacon.
4. Thread bacon rolls on 4 kabob skewers.
5. In a small bowl, combine soy sauce, oil and pepper.
6. Preheat broiler. Put kabobs on a broiler-pan rack. Spoon soy-sauce mixture over kabobs.
7. Broil 4 to 5 minutes. Turn kabobs; spoon remaining sauce over kabobs. Broil 4 to 5 minutes or until livers are done.
8. Serve kabobs with hot cooked rice or risotto and a green salad. Or, serve as an appetizer. Makes 4 main-dish servings.

Variation
Substitute calves' liver for chicken livers, if desired.

Brunch Kabobs

6 precooked sausage links, halved crosswise
8 oz. ham, cut in 1-inch chunks
16 button mushrooms
Vegetable oil
Freshly ground pepper
2 medium cooking apples, peeled, cut into 1/4-inch-thick rings
1/4 cup butter or margarine, melted
2 tablespoons sugar

1. Thread sausage, ham and mushrooms alternately on 4 kabob skewers.
2. Preheat broiler. Brush kabobs generously with oil; sprinkle with pepper.
3. Put kabobs on a broiler-pan rack. Broil about 3 minutes. Turn kabobs; broil 3 minutes more or until sausage is no longer pink.
4. Meanwhile, to make apple rings, in a large skillet, combine apples and melted butter or margarine. Cook over low heat 1 minute. Turn apple rings; increase heat to high. Sprinkle with sugar; cook 1 to 2 minutes.
5. Serve broiled kabobs over buttered apple rings. Makes 4 servings.

Scallops en Brochette

Salt
Freshly ground white pepper
6 tablespoons fresh bread crumbs
Finely grated peel of 1/2 lemon
1 lb. bay scallops
1 tablespoon all-purpose flour
Melted butter or margarine

Lemon-Cream Sauce:
1/2 cup whipping cream
Grated peel of 1/2 lemon
2 tablespoons finely chopped fresh parsley
Salt
Freshly ground pepper

1. Preheat broiler. In a shallow bowl, combine salt, white pepper, bread crumbs and lemon peel.
2. Coat scallops lightly in flour; dip coated scallops into melted butter or margarine. Roll buttered scallops in crumb mixture.
3. Thread on 4 kabob skewers. Place kabobs on a broiler-pan rack. Brush with additional melted butter or margarine.
4. Broil about 3 minutes. Turn kabobs; brush with additional melted butter or margarine. Broil 2 to 4 minutes or until scallops are done.
5. To make Lemon-Cream Sauce, in a small saucepan, heat cream until hot; stir in lemon peel and parsley. Season with salt and pepper. Serve sauce separately. Makes 4 servings.

Fish Kabobs

1 lb. firm-textured white fish, cod, halibut,
   monkfish, etc.
1/4 cup lime or lemon juice
6 tablespoons olive oil
Salt
Freshly ground pepper
1 tablespoon chopped fresh rosemary or
   1 teaspoon dried rosemary
4 small onions, cut into thick slices
1 lemon, cut into thin wedges

Use a firm-textured fish for kabobs to prevent fish falling apart during cooking. Fish kabobs keep their shape better if they are cooked on a baking sheet or large shallow pan, rather than a rack.

1. Cut fish into 1-inch cubes. Place fish cubes in a shallow dish.
2. In a small bowl, combine lime or lemon juice, olive oil, salt, pepper and rosemary. Spoon over fish. Cover; refrigerate 4 hours.
3. Preheat broiler. Thread marinated fish on 4 kabob skewers alternately with onion slices and lemon wedges. Place kabobs on a baking sheet or large shallow pan. Brush with marinade.
4. Broil 3 to 4 minutes. Turn kabobs; brush with marinade. Broil 3 to 4 minutes or until fish is cooked through.
5. Serve with warm pita bread and a green salad. Makes 4 servings.

Mixed Grill on a Skewer

8 oz. lamb, cut into 1-inch cubes
4 lamb's kidneys, skinned, quartered, cored
12 small cocktail sausages
12 button mushrooms

Basting Sauce:
1 tablespoon Worcestershire sauce
3 tablespoons chili sauce
2 tablespoons vegetable oil
1 garlic clove, crushed
Juice of 1/2 lemon
Salt
Freshly ground pepper

1. Thread lamb, kidneys, sausages and mushrooms alternately on 4 kabob skewers.
2. To make sauce, in a small bowl, combine sauce ingredients.
3. Preheat broiler. Put kabobs on a broiler-pan rack. Brush 1/2 of sauce over kabobs.
4. Broil 5 minutes.
5. Turn kabobs; brush with remaining sauce. Broil 5 minutes or until meats are tender.
6. Serve with sautéed potatoes and a green vegetable. Makes 4 servings.

Sole & Anchovy Roll-Ups

12 small sole fillets
Anchovy paste
All-purpose flour

Batter:
2/3 cup all-purpose flour
Salt
Freshly ground pepper
1 egg
1/2 cup milk
Vegetable oil for deep-frying

Parsley Mayonnaise:
1/2 cup mayonnaise
3 tablespoons dairy sour cream
3 tablespoons finely chopped fresh parsley

1. Cut each fillet in half crosswise.
2. Spread 1 side thinly with anchovy paste; roll up jelly-roll style.
3. Thread 6 sole rolls on each of 4 metal kabob skewers.
4. Dust lightly on all sides with flour.
5. To make batter, in a medium bowl, combine flour, salt and pepper. Stir in egg and a little milk. Beat in remaining milk until smooth.
6. Place kabobs in a long shallow dish without touching. Spoon batter over kabobs until coated.
7. Fill a long pan 1/3 full of oil; heat to 375F (190C) or until a 1-inch bread cube turns golden brown in 50 seconds. Carefully lower kabobs into hot oil. Deep-fry 5 to 6 minutes or until fish is crisp and golden. Remove kabobs with tongs; metal skewers will be hot. Drain kabobs on paper towels.
8. To make mayonnaise, in a small bowl combine mayonnaise, sour cream and parsley. Serve with hot kabobs. Makes 4 servings.

Clockwise from top: Mixed Grill on a Skewer, Fish Kabobs, Sole & Anchovy Roll-Ups with Parsley Mayonnaise

Grilled Chicken

2 (2-1/2- to 3-lb.) broiler-fryer chickens
6 tablespoons vegetable oil
1 tablespoon Worcestershire sauce
2 garlic cloves, crushed
Juice of 1/2 lemon
1 tablespoon prepared brown mustard
Salt
Freshly ground pepper

1. Place 1 chicken on a cutting board, breast-side down.
2. Cut through backbone with poultry shears or a sharp knife.
3. Remove backbone completely.
4. Open out chicken; place skin-side up on a cutting board. Pound with a meat mallet or rolling pin to flatten. Be careful not to splinter bones or tear flesh.
5. Fold wing tips under wings so they lie flat.
6. Insert 2 skewers, crisscross fashion, through chicken to hold it rigid. Repeat steps 1 through 6 for other chicken.
7. Place prepared chickens in a shallow dish.
8. In a small bowl, combine oil, Worcestershire sauce, garlic, lemon juice, mustard, salt and pepper. Spoon over chickens. Cover; refrigerate 4 to 6 hours, or preferably overnight.
9. Preheat grill. Place chickens, skin-side down, on grill rack. Grill 25 minutes.
10. Turn chickens; baste with remaining marinade. Grill 20 to 30 minutes or until tender. Makes 4 to 6 servings.

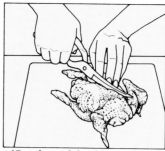

1/Cut through backbone with poultry shears or a sharp knife.

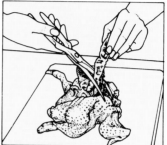

2/Remove backbone completely.

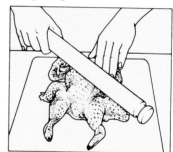

3/Pound with a meat mallet or rolling pin to flatten.

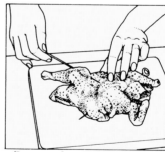

4/Insert 2 skewers, crisscross fashion, through each chicken to hold it rigid.

Grilled Chicken

Special Beef Kabobs

Marinade:
6 tablespoons vegetable oil
Grated peel of 1 orange
2 tablespoons brandy
2 tablespoons chopped fresh rosemary or
   2 teaspoons dried rosemary
1 garlic clove, crushed
Salt
Freshly ground pepper

Kabobs:
1 lb. lean beef, cut into 1-inch cubes
2 medium zucchini, about 8 oz., sliced
1 small orange, cut into 8 wedges

1. To make marinade, in a medium bowl, combine marinade ingredients.
2. Add beef to marinade; stir until coated. Cover; refrigerate 4 hours.
3. Remove beef from marinade; pat dry with paper towels.
4. Preheat broiler. Thread marinated beef on 4 kabob skewers alternately with zucchini and orange.
5. Place kabobs on a broiler-pan rack. Brush with marinade. Broil 5 to 6 minutes.
6. Turn kabobs; brush with additional marinade. Cook 5 to 6 minutes or to desired doneness.
7. Serve hot with rice and a green salad. Makes 4 servings.

Veal & Prune Kabobs

12 large pitted prunes
About 1/2 cup dry white wine
1-1/4 lb. lean veal, in 1 piece
3 ham slices
3 tablespoons honey
3 tablespoons white-wine vinegar
Salt
Freshly ground pepper
Vegetable oil

1. Place prunes in a shallow dish; add enough wine to cover. Let stand overnight or until plumped.
2. Cut veal into 1-inch cubes.
3. Cut each ham slice into 4 strips. Roll up each wine-soaked prune in a strip of ham.
4. Thread veal cubes and ham rolls on 4 kabob skewers.
5. Preheat broiler. In a small pan, heat honey and wine vinegar until honey dissolves. Season with salt and pepper.
6. Brush kabobs with oil; then brush with honey mixture.
7. Place kabobs on a broiler-pan rack. Broil about 6 minutes. Turn kabobs; brush with honey mixture. Broil 6 minutes or to desired doneness.
8. Serve hot. Makes 4 servings.

Pork Saté

3 tablespoons smooth or crunchy peanut butter
2 tablespoons soy sauce
1 tablespoon vinegar
1 tablespoon chicken stock or water
Salt
Freshly ground pepper
1 teaspoon curry powder
1 lb. pork-loin tenderloin

To serve:
2 lemons, cut into wedges

Saté are usually served as appetizers with drinks, or as part of an hors d'oeuvre. Use small bamboo or metal skewers.

1. In a small saucepan, combine peanut butter, soy sauce, vinegar, stock or water, salt, pepper and curry powder. Stir over low heat until blended. Set aside to cool.
2. Cut pork into 1/2-inch cubes.
3. Stir pork cubes into peanut-butter sauce. Cover; refrigerate 4 hours.
4. Preheat broiler. Thread marinated pork cubes on 12 small skewers. Place on a broiler-pan rack.
5. Broil about 2 minutes. Turn; broil 2 minutes more or until pork is no longer pink.
6. Serve with lemon wedges. Makes 6 servings.

Top to bottom: Pork Saté with peanut sauce, Special Beef Kabobs

Left to right: Ham & Cheese Kabobs, Skewered Meatballs

Ham & Cheese Kabobs

1 (12-oz.) 1-inch-thick cooked ham slice
8 oz. Edam cheese
All-purpose flour
1 egg, beaten
3 tablespoons fresh bread crumbs
Freshly ground pepper
1/4 cup red-currant jelly
Juice of 1/2 orange

1. Preheat broiler. Cut ham into 1-inch cubes.
2. Cut cheese into 3/4-inch cubes.
3. Dust cheese cubes lightly with flour. Dip floured cheese cubes into beaten egg; roll in bread crumbs until evenly coated.
4. Thread ham and coated cheese cubes alternately on 4 kabob skewers. Place on a broiler-pan rack; season with pepper.
5. In a small saucepan, combine jelly and orange juice. Stir over low heat until jelly melts. Spoon jelly mixture over kabobs.
6. Broil about 4 minutes. Turn kabobs; spoon over additional jelly mixture. Broil 4 minutes or until heated through.
7. Serve hot with Orange & Watercress Salad, page 12. Makes 4 servings.

Skewered Meatballs

1 lb. ground beef or lamb
1 medium onion, finely chopped
2 teaspoons fresh thyme or 1/2 teaspoon
  dried leaf thyme
Salt
Freshly ground pepper
2 garlic clove, crushed
2 egg yolks
1 large red bell pepper, halved
1 large green bell pepper, halved
5 tablespoons vegetable oil
1/8 teaspoon ground ginger
Pinch of ground turmeric

Yogurt & Cucumber Sauce:
1/2 cucumber, peeled, grated
1/2 teaspoon dill seeds
1/4 teaspoon sugar
1/2 cup plain yogurt
1 tablespoon chopped fresh mint

1. In a medium bowl, combine meat, onion, thyme, salt, pepper, garlic and egg yolks.
2. Shape into 24 small meatballs about the size of a walnut. Cover; refrigerate 3 to 4 hours to firm up texture of meatballs.
3. Cut bell peppers into 1-inch-square pieces.
4. Thread chilled meatballs and bell-pepper pieces alternately on 4 kabob skewers. Place kabobs into a shallow dish.
5. In a small bowl, combine oil, ginger, turmeric, salt and pepper. Brush kabobs with oil mixture. Cover; refrigerate 1 hour.
6. Preheat broiler.
7. To make sauce, squeeze grated cucumber in a dish towel to remove excess moisture. In a small bowl, combine cucumber, dill seeds, sugar, yogurt, mint, salt and pepper.
8. Place kabobs on a broiler-pan rack; brush with oil mixture. Broil 6 to 8 minutes.
9. Turn kabobs; brush with oil mixture. Broil 6 minutes or to desired doneness. Serve hot with sauce and a pasta salad. Makes 4 servings.

Special Sandwiches

Pumpernickel Party Snacks

1 (8-oz.) pkg. cream cheese, room temperature
1 tablespoon brandy
Freshly ground pepper
2 tablespoons finely chopped walnuts or almonds
36 pumpernickel or rye cocktail rounds

To garnish:
Black-grape halves or walnut halves

1. In a medium bowl, combine cream cheese, brandy, pepper and chopped nuts.
2. Spread 2/3 of rounds evenly with cheese mixture, reserving a little for securing garnish.
3. Assemble each sandwich, using 2 cheese-topped rounds and 1 plain round, placing plain round on top; see photo opposite.
4. Place a small amount of cheese mixture on top of each sandwich. Press a grape half or walnut half into cheese mixture.

Many sandwiches can be made ahead and frozen until needed. Most traditional fillings can be used. However, hard-cooked eggs and mayonnaise do not freeze well. Hard-cooked egg whites become rubbery when frozen; mayonnaise separates. Sandwiches that are packed frozen for a picnic will thaw in time for lunch.

Vary the types of breads, spreads and fillings to make sandwiches more interesting. Choose breads and fillings that complement each other. For example, robust, sturdy bread goes well with sausages and cheese. Choose a bread with a more delicate flavor and texture for chicken-salad sandwiches. Seasoned butters make excellent spreads, or try one of the many mustards on the market. Let your imagination take charge!

Salami & Pita Specials

4 pita-bread rounds
2 to 3 cups shredded lettuce
1 medium onion, chopped
Olive oil
6 oz. feta cheese or mozzarella cheese, cubed
4 oz. salami, thinly sliced
1/4 cup pitted black olives, chopped
Freshly ground pepper

---

1. Preheat oven to 350F (175C). Wrap pita bread loosely in foil. Heat in preheated oven 5 minutes.
2. Cut each pita to form a pocket.
3. Fill pockets with a layer of lettuce and a little chopped onion. Drizzle a little olive oil over lettuce and onion.
4. Add some cheese, salami and olives to each pocket. Season with pepper. Work quickly so bread does not cool.
5. Serve while bread is still warm. Makes 4 sandwiches.

Smoked-Salmon Rarebit

2 cups shredded Swiss cheese (8 oz.)
2 eggs, separated
1 teaspoon prepared brown mustard
Freshly ground pepper
3 tablespoons milk
3 oz. smoked-salmon trimmings, finely chopped
4 whole-wheat-bread slices

To garnish:
Lemon slices
Fresh parsley sprigs

---

1. Preheat broiler. In a medium bowl, combine cheese, egg yolks, mustard, pepper, milk and smoked salmon.
2. In a medium bowl, beat egg whites until stiff but not dry. Fold beaten egg whites into cheese mixture.
3. Toast bread on 1 side only.
4. Divide cheese mixture among 4 bread slices, spreading evenly on untoasted side of bread.
5. Broil under preheated broiler until cheese topping puffs and is golden brown.
6. Serve hot. Makes 4 servings.

Clockwise from top: Pumpernickel Party Snacks, Smoked-Salmon Rarebit, Salami & Pita Specials

Smorgasbord Pinwheel

1 bread loaf, 9 or 10 inches in diameter
Butter or margarine, room temperature
2 (8-oz.) pkgs. cream cheese, room temperature
4 oz. blue cheese, crumbled, room temperature
Freshly ground pepper
3 tablespoons mayonnaise
1 (3-oz.) jar red lumpfish caviar
1 (3-oz.) jar black lumpfish caviar
About 1 cup sliced pimento-stuffed olives

---

1. Cut 1 (3/4-inch-thick) slice from widest part of loaf. Spread bread slice with a thin layer of butter or margarine. Place buttered bread on a flat board or platter.
2. In a medium bowl, beat 1/2 of cream cheese until creamy. Beat in blue cheese and pepper.
3. Spread blue-cheese mixture evenly over buttered bread.
4. In a medium bowl, beat remaining cream cheese and mayonnaise.
5. Mark cheese-topped bread into 8 equal sections with a knife blade.
6. Fill a pastry bag fitted with a star tip with mayonnaise-and-cheese mixture. Pipe mixture into rosettes along marked lines and around outer edge of circle.
7. Fill 4 alternate sections with sliced olives. Fill 2 opposite sections with red caviar; fill remaining 2 sections with black caviar. See photo opposite. Makes 8 servings.

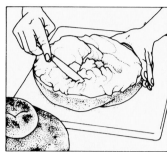

1/Spread blue-cheese mixture evenly over buttered bread.

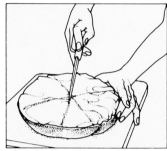

2/Mark cheese-topped bread into 8 equal sections with a knife blade.

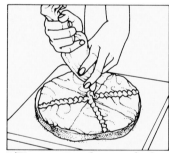

3/Pipe rosettes along marked lines and around outer edge of circle.

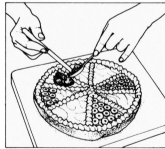

4/Fill sections with sliced olives, red caviar and black caviar. See photo opposite.

Smorgasbord Pinwheel

Fishermen's Sticks

12 fish sticks
Butter or margarine, melted
6 long crusty rolls
Ketchup
2 small pkgs. potato chips, coarsely crushed
3 tomatoes, cut into thin wedges

This makes an excellent party snack for older children. The rolls look appetizing and are easy to eat. I have yet to meet a child who does not like fish sticks!

1. Preheat broiler. Brush fish sticks with butter or margarine. Place under preheated broiler. Broil 8 to 10 minutes, turning once. Keep warm.
2. Preheat oven to 375F (190C). Split rolls lengthwise; do not cut all the way through. Brush inside each roll with butter or margarine. Place buttered rolls on a baking sheet. Bake in preheated oven 5 minutes.
3. Spread buttered surface of warm rolls with ketchup. Fill each roll with a layer of potato chips, 2 broiled fish sticks and tomato wedges. Serve immediately. Makes 6 servings.

Avocados, sometimes called alligator pears, originally came from Central America. To choose avocados, look for ones that are firm and free from cuts and bruises. The avocado should yield slightly when pressed. If it is too hard, it may rot rather than ripen. Ripen avocados at room temperature for two to three days. After cutting the avocado, sprinkle with lime or lemon juice to prevent browning. If you are only using half of the avocado, sprinkle the remaining half with lime or lemon juice; refrigerate with the seed still in place.

Baked Sardine Toasts

2 eggs
1 tablespoon Worcestershire sauce
Salt
Freshly ground pepper
4 bread slices
2 (7-oz.) cans sardines in oil
Grated peel of 1/2 lemon
8 oz. cream cheese with chives
2 tablespoons mayonnaise
1 small onion, finely chopped

1. Preheat oven to 375F (190C). Grease a baking sheet. In a medium bowl, beat eggs, Worcestershire sauce, salt and pepper.
2. Dip both sides of bread slices into egg mixture. Place dipped bread on greased baking sheet. Bake in preheated oven 5 minutes.
3. Drain oil from sardines; mash sardines with lemon peel and pepper. Spread evenly over each slice of baked bread.
4. In a medium bowl, beat cream cheese with a wooden spoon to soften; beat in mayonnaise and onion. Spread cheese mixture evenly over sardine mixture.
5. Bake in preheated oven 15 minutes or until topping is golden. Serve immediately. Makes 4 servings.

Avocado & Shrimp Rolls

4 whole-wheat rolls
Butter or margarine, room temperature
1 ripe avocado, halved
Juice of 1 lemon
Salt
Freshly ground black pepper
6 oz. deveined, peeled, cooked shrimp
1/4 cup mayonnaise
Red (cayenne) pepper
Lettuce leaves

1. Cut each roll in half crosswise.
2. Spread 1 cut surface of each layer with butter or margarine.
3. Cut avocado into thin slices. In a small bowl, toss avocado slices in lemon juice. Season with salt and black pepper.
4. In a medium bowl, combine shrimp, mayonnaise, a little red pepper, salt and pepper.
5. Divide avocado slices, shrimp mixture and lettuce among roll bottoms. Sandwich together with roll tops. Makes 4 servings.

Smoked-Haddock Triangles

1 lb. smoked haddock
Milk
1 bay leaf
Freshly ground pepper
About 1/2 cup mayonnaise
Grated peel of 1 lemon
8 white-bread slices
4 whole-wheat-bread slices
Butter, room temperature
Chopped fresh parsley

To garnish:
Small lemon fans

1. Place fish in a shallow pan. Add enough milk to half cover; add bay leaf and pepper. Simmer until fish is tender.
2. Drain fish, discarding milk and bay leaf. Discard any skin and bone; flake flesh. Cool.
3. In a small bowl, combine flaked fish with enough mayonnaise to bind. Stir in lemon peel.
4. Spread 1 side of each white-bread slice and both sides of whole-wheat-bread slices evenly with butter or margarine.
5. For each sandwich, spread 1/8 of fish mixture on buttered side of 1 white-bread slice and 1 whole-wheat-bread slice. Place whole-wheat-bread slice over topping on white bread. Top with an untopped white-bread slice, buttered-side down. Repeat to make 4 sandwiches.
6. Cut off crusts; cut each sandwich into 4 triangles.
7. Spread tops of each triangle lightly with mayonnaise; sprinkle with chopped parsley.
8. Garnish triangles with lemon fans. Makes 16 triangles.

Left to right: Baked Sardine Toasts, Smoked-Haddock Triangles

Beef & Coleslaw Sandwich

3 hot toast slices
Butter or margarine, room temperature
10 to 12 thin cucumber slices
2 tablespoons coleslaw
Prepared horseradish
2 rare roast-beef slices

To garnish:
Radish slices
Pickled onion
Sweet pickle

1. Spread 1 side of each toast slice with butter or margarine.
2. Top 1 buttered side of toast with a layer of cucumber and coleslaw, reserving 1 cucumber slice for garnish. Spread buttered side of 1 piece of toast with horseradish. Place horseradish-side up on first layer.
3. Arrange beef slices on horseradish; place third slice of toast on top, buttered-side down.
4. Cut sandwich in half diagonally; garnish 1 sandwich half with radish slices and reserved cucumber slice; garnish remaining half with pickle and onion. Makes 1 serving.

Blue-Cheese Special

2 whole-wheat-bread slices
Butter or margarine, room temperature
1/2 cup crumbled blue cheese (2 oz.)
2 crisp-cooked bacon slices, crumbled
1 tablespoon mayonnaise
Freshly ground pepper

1. Preheat broiler. Spread 1 side of both bread slices with butter or margarine.
2. Place 1 bread slice, buttered-side down, on a broiler-pan rack.
3. In a small bowl, combine blue cheese, bacon, mayonnaise and pepper.
4. Spread cheese mixture evenly over bread slice on rack. Top with remaining slice, buttered-side up. Press bread gently together.
5. Broil sandwich under preheated broiler 4 to 5 minutes, turning sandwich once.
6. Serve immediately. Makes 1 sandwich.

Pâté Beehives

14 whole-wheat-bread slices
12 oz. liver pâté
Butter or margarine, melted
1/4 cup chopped fresh parsley
1/4 cup chopped toasted nuts
2 pimento-stuffed olives, sliced

These attractive sandwiches are made of 3 layers of bread each. Each layer is a different diameter. You should be able to get 1 (2-1/2-inch) circle from 1 slice of bread, 2 (2-inch) circles from 1 slice and 4 (1-1/2-inch) circles from 1 slice.

1. Cut 8 (2-1/2-inch) bread circles, 8 (2-inch) bread circles and 8 (1-1/2-inch) bread circles.
2. Spread large circles with 2/3 of pâté; spread medium circles with remaining pâté.
3. To assemble beehives, place a medium circle on top of each large circle; top with a small circle. See illustration below.
4. Smooth edges, using a round-bladed knife. Refrigerate 20 minutes.
5. Brush beehives with melted butter or margarine. Roll 4 beehives in chopped parsley; roll remaining beehives in toasted nuts.
6. Top each coated beehive with an olive slice. Makes 8 sandwiches.

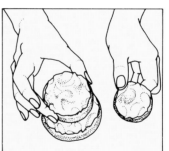

1/To assemble beehives, place a medium circle on top of each large circle; top with a small circle.

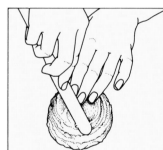

2/Smooth edges, using a round-bladed knife.

Left to right: Beef & Coleslaw Sandwich, Pâté Beehives

Left to right: Chicken & Almond Rounds, Toasted Ham & Cheese Sandwich, Toasted Tuna & Egg Sandwich, Toasted Chicken Sandwich

Chicken & Almond Rounds

16 whole-wheat-bread slices
Butter or margarine, room temperature
3/4 cup finely chopped cooked chicken
2 tablespoons dairy sour cream
1/4 cup chopped toasted almonds
Salt
Freshly ground pepper
About 1/4 cup red-currant jelly

1. Cut 1 (3-1/2-inch) circle from each bread slice using a fluted pastry cutter.
2. Cut a 1-inch center from 1/2 of circles to make rings.
3. Spread 1 side of each circle and ring with butter or margarine.
4. In a small bowl, combine chicken, sour cream, almonds, salt and pepper.
5. Spread circles with chicken mixture; top with rings.
6. Place 1 teaspoon jelly into center of each sandwich. Makes 8 sandwiches.

Toasted Ham & Cheese Sandwich

2 white-bread slices
Butter or margarine, room temperature
Prepared brown mustard
1/2 cup shredded Cheddar cheese (2 oz.)
1 ham slice (2 oz.)
Freshly ground pepper

1. Preheat broiler. Spread 1 side of both slices of bread thinly with butter or margarine; spread unbuttered side with a thin layer of mustard.
2. Place 1 bread slice, buttered-side down, on a broiler-pan rack.
3. Place 1/2 of cheese on bread on rack. Top with ham, remaining cheese and pepper.
4. Top with remaining bread, buttered-side up. Press sandwich gently together.
5. Broil sandwich under preheated broiler 4 to 5 minutes, turning sandwich once.
6. Serve immediately. Makes 1 sandwich.

Toasted Tuna & Egg Sandwich

2 white-bread slices
Butter or margarine, room temperature
1 hard-cooked egg, chopped
1 green onion, chopped
Salt
Freshly ground pepper
2 tablespoons tuna
2 tablespoons mayonnaise

1. Preheat broiler. Spread both sides of bread with butter or margarine.
2. Place 1 bread slice on a broiler-pan rack.
3. In a small bowl, combine egg, onion, salt, pepper, tuna and mayonnaise.
4. Spread egg mixture evenly over bread on rack; top with remaining slice. Press sandwich gently together.
5. Broil sandwich under preheated broiler 4 to 5 minutes, turning sandwich once.
6. Serve immediately. Makes 1 sandwich.

Toasted Chicken Sandwich

2 whole-wheat-bread slices
Butter or margarine, room temperature
1/2 cup chopped cooked chicken
1 tablespoon mayonnaise
2 tablespoons corn relish
1 tablespoon finely chopped celery
Salt
Freshly ground pepper

1. Preheat broiler. Spread both sides of bread with butter or margarine.
2. Place 1 bread slice on a broiler-pan rack.
3. In a small bowl, combine chicken, mayonnaise, corn relish, celery, salt and pepper.
4. Spread chicken mixture evenly over bread on rack. Top with remaining slice. Press sandwich gently together.
5. Broil sandwich under preheated broiler 4 to 5 minutes, turning sandwich once.
6. Serve immediately. Makes 1 sandwich.

Frankfurter & Onion Delight

1 tablespoon vegetable oil
1 small onion, peeled, cut into thin rings
2 white-bread slices
Butter or margarine, room temperature
1 frankfurter, cut into thin slices
1 tablespoon chopped pickle
Freshly ground pepper

1. Preheat broiler. Heat oil in a small skillet. Add onion; sauté until tender and lightly golden.
2. Spread 1 side of both bread slices with butter or margarine.
3. Place 1 slice of bread, buttered-side down, on a broiler-pan rack.
4. In a small bowl, combine cooked onion, frankfurter, pickle and pepper.
5. Spread frankfurter mixture evenly over bread on rack. Top with remaining slice, buttered-side up. Press sandwich gently together.
6. Broil sandwich under preheated broiler 4 to 5 minutes, turning sandwich once.
7. Serve immediately. Makes 1 sandwich.

Cheesy-Potato Burgers

4 (4-oz.) ground beef patties
Vegetable oil
2 hamburger buns
1/4 cup ketchup
Salt
Freshly ground pepper
1 cup mashed potatoes
1 cup shredded Cheddar cheese (4 oz.)

1. Preheat broiler. Place beef patties on a broiler-pan rack. Broil under preheated broiler 3 minutes per side or to desired doneness.
2. Separate buns in half. Lightly toast buns.
3. Spread buns with ketchup; top each with a broiled hamburger. Season with salt and pepper.
4. Preheat oven to 375F (190C). In a small bowl, combine mashed potatoes and cheese. Spread potato mixture over hamburgers.
5. Bake in preheated oven 15 minutes or until potato topping is golden.
6. Serve hot. Makes 4 servings.

Steak & Egg Toast

2 tablespoons butter or margarine
1 beef cube steak, about 4 oz.
Salt
Freshly ground pepper
2 bread slices
1 or 2 teaspoons vegetable oil
1 egg
Prepared brown mustard

To garnish:
Watercress

A perfect sandwich to choose when you are on your own. This is an excellent way to pamper yourself.

1. Melt butter or margarine in a skillet. Add steak; sauté about 3 minutes on each side for medium done or to desired doneness.
2. Season steak with salt and pepper. Keep warm.
3. Cut crusts from bread; toast until golden.
4. In a small skillet, heat enough oil to keep egg from sticking. Add egg; cook until set.
5. Spread 1 toast slice with mustard. Top with steak, fried egg and remaining toast.
6. Garnish with watercress; serve immediately. Makes 1 sandwich.

Variation
Substitute any thin, tender beef steak for cube steak. Some markets sell a breakfast steak that is ideal.

Clockwise from top: Cheesy-Potato Burgers, Steak & Egg Toast, Frankfurter & Onion Delight

Individual Boeuf en Croûte

4 (1/2-inch-thick) beef-loin tenderloin steaks
1/2 cup red wine
Salt
Freshly ground pepper
1 garlic clove, crushed
1/4 cup butter or margarine
3 oz. mushrooms, chopped
1 (17-1/2-oz.) pkg. puff pastry, thawed, if frozen
3 oz. liver pâté, cut into 4 slices
1 egg, beaten

1. Place steaks in a shallow dish. Add wine, salt, pepper and garlic.
2. Cover; refrigerate overnight.
3. Pat steaks dry with paper towels.
4. Melt butter or margarine in a skillet. Add steaks; sauté 1 to 2 minutes on each side. Cool steaks.
5. Preheat oven to 400F (205C). Grease a baking sheet.
6. Add mushrooms to fat remaining in skillet; cook 2 to 3 minutes. Drain mushrooms.
7. Cut each pastry sheet in half. On a lightly floured surface, roll out each half to a piece large enough to enclose 1 steak.
8. Put a cooled steak in center of each pastry piece. Top with 1/4 of mushrooms and a pâté slice.
9. Brush pastry edges with beaten egg. Wrap pastry around steak. Trim off excess pastry; reserve. Pinch edges to seal. Repeat with remaining pastry, steaks, mushrooms and pâté.
10. Place on greased baking sheet; brush with egg to glaze.
11. Roll out pastry trimmings; cut small leaves for decoration. Arrange leaves on pastry; brush with egg.
12. Bake in preheated oven 25 minutes or until pastry is puffed and golden.
13. Serve hot or cold. Makes 4 servings.

Spaghetti al Cartoccio

8 oz. spaghetti
1/4 cup butter or margarine
2 garlic cloves, minced
1/2 lb. uncooked shrimp, peeled, deveined
1/2 pint whipping cream (1 cup)
1/4 lb. smoked-salmon trimmings, coarsely chopped
4 anchovy fillets, drained, chopped
1 (8-3/4-oz.) jar mussels, drained
1/2 cup grated Parmesan cheese
Freshly ground pepper

This pasta dish can be served as a first course or as a light main dish accompanied by a salad.

1. Cook spaghetti in lightly salted boiling water about 10 minutes or until almost tender. Drain well; return to saucepan. Set aside.
2. Melt butter or margarine in a medium saucepan. Add garlic and shrimp; cook 2 minutes. Stir in cream, smoked salmon, anchovies and mussels. Stirring gently, cook 2 to 3 minutes or until heated through. Remove from heat; stir in cheese and pepper. Pour sauce over spaghetti; toss to combine.
3. Preheat oven to 400F (205C). Cut 2 large sheets of parchment paper; place in a double layer on a 15" x 10" jelly-roll pan. Crinkle papers around outer edges; turn up slightly to make a large bag. Spoon spaghetti into bag. Pull opposite sides of paper over spaghetti; staple closed. Pull remaining sides of paper over; staple closed.
4. Bake in preheated oven 12 to 15 minutes or until paper is puffed.
5. Place on a serving plate. Carefully remove staples; open to release the wonderful aroma. Serve immediately from paper dish. Makes 8 first-course servings or 4 light main-dish servings.

Top to bottom: Spaghetti al Cartoccio, Individual Boeuf en Croûte

Beef & Rice Koulabiac

1 tablespoon butter or margarine
1 medium onion, finely chopped
8 oz. lean ground beef
1 garlic clove, crushed
3/4 cup cooked white rice
Salt
Freshly ground pepper
2 tablespoons sherry
2 tablespoons whipping cream
2 tablespoons chopped fresh parsley
1 hard-cooked egg, finely chopped
1 (17-1/2-oz.) pkg. puff pastry, thawed, if frozen
1 egg, beaten

Egg Sauce:
2 hard-cooked eggs
1 teaspoon prepared brown mustard
Juice of 1/2 lemon
1/2 cup olive oil
1 tablespoon chopped fresh chives

1. Melt butter or margarine in a large skillet. Add onion; sauté 2 to 3 minutes.
2. Add meat; sauté 5 minutes or until no longer pink. Drain off excess fat.
3. Stir in garlic, cooked rice, salt, pepper, sherry and cream. Cook 1 minute, stirring constantly.
4. Stir in parsley and chopped hard-cooked egg; cool.
5. Overlap 2 sheets of puff pastry into 1 sheet, brushing edge with water. On a lightly floured surface, roll out pastry to a 14-inch square.
6. Spoon meat mixture into center of pastry.
7. Brush pastry edges with beaten egg. Fold corners of pastry to center. Pinch pastry edges together to seal, completely enclosing filling.
8. Place on greased baking sheet; refrigerate 20 minutes.
9. Preheat oven to 425F (220C). Brush pastry with beaten egg to glaze. Bake in preheated oven 30 to 35 minutes or until pastry is puffed and golden.
10. To make sauce, separate hard-cooked eggs. Sieve yolks; chop whites finely. In a small bowl, combine sieved yolks, mustard and lemon juice. Gradually beat in olive oil; season with salt and pepper. Stir in chopped egg whites and chives.
11. Serve sauce with hot koulabiac. Makes 4 servings.

Crepes

2 cups all-purpose flour
1/4 teaspoon salt
4 eggs
1 pint milk (2 cups)
1/4 cup butter or margarine, melted
Butter or margarine for cooking

1. In a large bowl, combine flour and salt. In a medium bowl, with a whisk, beat eggs; beat in milk until combined. Slowly pour egg mixture into flour, beating constantly. Beat until mixture is blended and batter is smooth. Slowly add melted butter or margarine, beating until combined.
2. Or, place ingredients in a blender or food processor. Process 1 to 2 minutes or until batter is smooth.
3. Pour batter into a pitcher. Cover and refrigerate at least 1 hour.
4. Stir refrigerated batter. If batter has thickened slightly, stir in a few teaspoons of milk.
5. Melt 1 teaspoon butter or margarine in a 6- or 7-inch skillet or crepe pan over medium heat. Pour in 3 tablespoons batter or enough to make a thin layer in bottom pan. Cook over medium heat 1-1/2 minutes or until small bubbles begin to form on crepe's surface. With a spatula, turn crepe over; cook 1-1/2 minutes. Remove cooked crepe to a flat plate; repeat with remaining batter. Add more butter or margarine to skillet or pan as necessary.
6. Cool crepes. Refrigerate up to 2 days or freeze. Makes about 34 crepes.

Chicken Crepes

2 tablespoons butter or margarine
2 tablespoons all-purpose flour
1 cup milk
1 cup shredded Swiss cheese (4 oz.)
Salt
Freshly ground pepper
1 cup chopped cooked chicken
1/4 cup chopped walnuts, almonds or pecans
1 tablespoon chopped fresh parsley
8 crepes, recipe above

1. Melt butter or margarine in a medium saucepan over medium heat. Stir in flour; cook 1 minute, stirring constantly. Slowly stir in milk; cook until slightly thickened, stirring constantly. Stir in cheese until melted. Season with salt and pepper. Stir in chicken, nuts and parsley.
2. Preheat oven to 350F (175C). Grease a 13" x 9" baking dish.
3. Spoon 1-1/2 tablespoons chicken mixture onto each crepe. Fold crepe over filling. Place filled crepes, seam-side down, in greased baking dish.
4. Cover with foil. Bake in preheated oven 15 to 20 minutes or until heated through.
5. Serve immediately. Makes 4 servings, 2 crepes each.

Frankfurter & Beans in Bundles

1 tablespoon vegetable oil
4 frankfurters
1 (8-oz.) pkg. refrigerator crescent-roll dough
1 egg, beaten
1 (15-oz.) can baked beans in tomato sauce
2 tablespoons grated Parmesan cheese

1. Preheat oven to 375F (190C). Grease a baking sheet.
2. Heat oil in a skillet. Add frankfurters; sauté 3 to 4 minutes, turning from time to time. Drain on paper towels.
3. Separate dough into 4 rectangles; press to seal perforations. On a lightly floured surface, roll each rectangle to a 8" x 6" rectangle. Or, roll rectangles large enough to cover frankfurters and beans.
4. Brush edges of pastry rectangles with beaten egg.
5. Lay a sautéed frankfurter on each pastry rectangle; add about 1/3 cup beans. Fold pastry over frankfurters and beans; pinch pastry edges together to seal.
6. Place on greased baking sheet; brush with beaten egg to glaze. Sprinkle with Parmesan cheese.
7. Bake in preheated oven 20 minutes or until golden brown. Makes 4 servings.

Top to bottom: Chicken Crepes, Beef & Rice Koulabiac with Egg Sauce

Garlic Chicken in Cabbage Leaves

1/4 cup butter or margarine, room temperature
3 tablespoons chopped fresh parsley
2 large garlic cloves, crushed
Salt
Freshly ground pepper
4 chicken drumsticks, boned
8 large cabbage leaves
About 1/2 cup white wine

---

1. In a small bowl, combine butter or margarine, 2 tablespoons parsley, garlic, salt and pepper.
2. Spoon 1/4 of flavored butter or margarine into cavity of each drumstick. Wrap in plastic wrap; refrigerate 1 hour to firm filling.
3. Preheat oven to 350F (175C). Cut away tough stalk from each cabbage leaf. Place in boiling water; blanch 1 minute. Place in a bowl of cold water.
4. Drain blanched cabbage leaves on paper towels.
5. Wrap each chilled drumstick in 2 cabbage leaves. Place in a shallow ovenproof dish.
6. Pour 1/2 cup wine over cabbage rolls. Season with salt, pepper and remaining parsley. Cover dish with foil.
7. Bake in preheated oven 40 minutes or until chicken is tender when pierced with a skewer, adding additional wine if necessary.
8. Uncover dish; serve immediately. Makes 4 servings.

Duck with Apricot & Cherry Sauce

4 duck quarters, 10 to 12 oz. each
Salt
Freshly ground pepper
1 (7-oz.) can apricot halves in light syrup
1 (15-oz.) can dark sweet cherries, drained

---

1. Preheat oven to 400F (205C).
2. Prick duck quarters all over with a fork or skewer. Sprinkle with salt and pepper.
3. Place seasoned duck on a roasting rack in a roasting pan.
4. Bake in preheated oven 40 minutes. Allow duck to cool slightly.
5. In a blender or food processor fitted with a steel blade, process apricots and syrup until blended.
6. Stir cherries into apricot puree.
7. Place each baked duck quarter in center of a foil square large enough to completely enclose it, shiny-side up. Pull up foil edges.
8. Spoon fruit sauce over duck. Pinch foil edges together to seal.
9. Bake in preheated oven 20 to 25 minutes. Open one package to test that duck is tender.
10. Serve hot. Makes 4 servings.

Baked Pork & Red-Cabbage Rolls

4 pork chops, trimmed
1/4 cup applesauce
1 tablespoon chopped fresh sage or 1 teaspoon
   dried leaf sage
Salt
Freshly ground pepper
8 large red-cabbage leaves
2/3 cup unsweetened apple juice

To garnish:
Raw apple slices tossed in lemon juice, if desired

---

1. Preheat broiler. Place pork chops on a broiler-pan rack. Broil 3 minutes per side. Cool slightly.
2. Spread 1 side of each broiled pork chop with applesauce. Sprinkle with sage, salt and pepper.
3. Cut any tough stalk from cabbage leaves. Place in boiling water; blanch 2 minutes. Place in a bowl of cold water.
4. Drain blanched cabbage leaves on paper towels.
5. Preheat oven to 350F (175C). Wrap each pork chop in 2 cabbage leaves. Place in a shallow ovenproof dish.
6. Pour over apple juice. Cover dish with foil.
7. Bake in preheated oven 1 hour or until pork chops are tender when pierced with a knife.
8. Garnish with apple slices, if desired. Makes 4 servings.

Top to bottom: Baked Pork & Red-Cabbage Rolls, Duck with Apricot & Cherry Sauce

Stuffed Onions

4 large onions, peeled
Water
6 bacon slices, chopped
3 tablespoons chopped fresh parsley
1/4 cup fresh bread crumbs
1 egg, beaten
2 tablespoons grated Parmesan cheese
Salt
Freshly ground pepper

To serve:
Seasoned tomato sauce or mushroom sauce

1. Preheat oven to 375F (190C). Grease a baking dish large enough to hold onions in 1 layer.
2. Carefully hollow out onions, using a grapefruit knife, leaving shells about 1/2 inch thick; reserve onion pieces.
3. Place onions in a large saucepan. Add enough water to cover; bring to a boil. Boil 6 minutes.
4. Finely chop pieces from onion centers.
5. Place bacon in a skillet over medium heat. Sauté until fat starts to run. Add chopped onions; sauté 3 minutes.
6. In a medium bowl, combine cooked onion mixture, parsley, bread crumbs, egg, cheese, salt and pepper.
7. Spoon stuffing mixture into each onion shell.
8. Place onions in greased baking dish; cover with foil.
9. Bake in preheated oven 1 hour or until onions are tender when pierced with a fork.
10. Serve with a simple tomato or mushroom sauce, if desired. Makes 4 servings.

Top to bottom: Mustard Baked Trout, Sole & Spinach Rolls with Lemon Sauce

Mustard Baked Trout

4 trout, ready for cooking
Vegetable oil
3 tablespoons butter or margarine
1 small onion, finely chopped
1 garlic clove, crushed
3 tablespoons all-purpose flour
1/2 cup milk
1/2 cup chicken stock
1 tablespoon prepared horseradish mustard
Salt
Freshly ground pepper

To garnish:
Chopped parsley

---

1. Preheat oven to 375F (190C). Fillet trout, if desired.
2. Cut 4 rectangular pieces of foil, each large enough to completely enclose a trout. Brush each foil piece with oil. Pull up foil edges; lay a trout along center of each foil piece.
3. To make sauce, in a medium saucepan, melt butter or margarine. Add onion; sauté 3 minutes. Stir in garlic and flour; cook 1 minute.
4. Gradually stir in milk and stock.
5. Bring to a boil; stir in mustard, salt and pepper. Simmer sauce 5 minutes, stirring frequently.
6. Spoon sauce over each trout.
7. Pull edges of foil up and over trout, folding edges together to seal. Place foil packages on a baking sheet.
8. Bake in preheated oven 25 minutes or until fish tests done. Check for doneness by carefully opening 1 package.
9. To serve, carefully fold back foil. Garnish with chopped parsley, if desired. Serve immediately. Makes 4 servings.

Sole & Spinach Rolls

4 large sole fillets, skinned
12 anchovy fillets
Freshly ground pepper
2 tablespoons chopped fresh parsley
Grated peel of 1/2 lemon
12 medium fresh spinach leaves
6 tablespoons butter or margarine, melted

Lemon Sauce:
1/2 cup mayonnaise
3 tablespoons whipping cream
Grated peel of 1 lemon

---

1. On a work surface, lay sole fillets out flat.
2. Arrange 3 anchovy fillets on each sole fillet. Sprinkle with pepper, parsley and lemon peel.
3. Roll up fillets. Secure with wooden picks; refrigerate 30 minutes.
4. Preheat oven to 400F (205C). Grease a baking dish large enough to hold rolled fillets in 1 layer.
5. Place spinach in boiling water. Blanch 30 seconds. Place in a bowl of iced water. Drain on paper towels. On a work surface, spread out blanched leaves.
6. Remove wooden picks from each rolled fillet; roll each fillet in 3 spinach leaves.
7. Place sole-and-spinach rolls in greased baking dish. Spoon over melted butter or margarine.
8. Cover dish. Bake in preheated oven 15 minutes or until fish tests done.
9. To make sauce, place mayonnaise, cream and lemon peel in the top of a double boiler over simmering water. Stir until heated. Serve sauce separately with cooked fish. Makes 4 servings.

Lamb en Croûte

6 tablespoons butter or margarine, room temperature
Grated peel of 1 lemon
1 garlic clove, crushed
1 tablespoon chopped fresh parsley
Salt
Freshly ground pepper
6 large lamb chops
Pastry for a double-crust pie
1 egg, slightly beaten

If you prefer lamb well-done, cook until partly done and cool before wrapping in pastry.

1. In a small bowl, combine butter or margarine, lemon peel, garlic, parsley, salt and pepper.
2. Roll flavored butter or margarine into a 1-inch diameter roll in a piece of waxed paper. Refrigerate until firm.
3. Preheat oven to 375F (190C). Grease a baking sheet. Season lamb with salt and pepper.
4. Cut pastry in half. On a lightly floured surface, roll out 1 pastry half into a piece large enough to enclose 3 lamb chops. Cut into 3 pieces. Repeat with remaining pastry.
5. Cut butter or margarine into 6 slices; place 1 slice in center of each pastry piece.
6. Place a chop over butter or margarine; wrap pastry over chop, so that it is completely enclosed. Trim off excess pastry; press edges to seal.
7. Place on greased baking sheet; brush with egg. Roll pastry trimmings; cut out small shapes for decoration, if desired. Place decorations on pastry; brush with egg.
8. Bake in preheated oven 35 to 40 minutes or until pastry is golden brown. Lamb will still be pink.
9. Serve hot with green vegetables. Makes 6 servings.

Left to right: Lamb en Croûte, Individual Apple-Apricot Strudels

Individual Apple-Apricot Strudels

8 dried apricots, coarsely chopped
1 large tart apple, peeled, cored, thinly sliced
1/3 cup raisins
1 tablespoon lemon juice
1 teaspoon grated lemon peel
1/3 cup firmly packed brown sugar
1/2 teaspoon pumpkin-pie spice
8 filo-dough sheets
1/4 cup butter or margarine, melted
Powdered sugar

1. In a medium bowl, combine apricots, apple, raisins, lemon juice, lemon peel, brown sugar and pumpkin-pie spice. Set aside.
2. Preheat oven to 400F (205C).
3. Unfold filo dough; lay flat between 2 slightly dampened dish towels. Cut a large sheet of waxed paper; place on a flat work surface. Place 1 filo sheet on waxed paper; brush with melted butter or margarine. Cover with a second filo sheet; brush with melted butter or margarine. Repeat with 2 more filo sheets and more butter or margarine. Cut filo layers in half lengthwise to make 2 (12" x 8") rectangles. Repeat with 4 remaining filo sheets.
4. Spoon 1/4 of apple mixture on center of each rectangle. Fold long sides of filo over filling. Fold opposite ends of filo up and over filling, envelope-style. Brush with melted butter or margarine. Place strudels, seam-side down, on an ungreased baking sheet.
5. Bake in preheated oven 18 to 20 minutes or until strudels are puffed and golden. Cool on baking sheet 5 minutes.
6. Dust with powdered sugar; serve warm. Makes 4 servings.

Hot Fruit Salad

1 large firm banana, cut into 4 chunks
2 eating apples, cored, cut into thick wedges
1 large firm pear, peeled, cored, cut into wedges
Juice of 1 lemon
1 cup green grapes
4 small plums, halved
1/4 cup butter or margarine
1/3 cup packed brown sugar
2 tablespoons sherry
1/4 teaspoon pumpkin-pie spice

To serve:
Whipping cream or ice cream

1. Preheat oven to 375F (190C). In a medium bowl, combine banana, apples, pear, lemon juice, grapes and plums.
2. Cut 4 (8-inch) foil squares; shape foil into foil cups. Fill cups with fruit mixture.
3. In a small saucepan, combine butter or margarine, brown sugar, sherry and spice. Stir over low heat until sugar dissolves.
4. Spoon sugar mixture over fruit.
5. Pull foil edges up and over fruit; fold edges together to seal. Place foil packages on a baking sheet.
6. Bake in preheated oven 20 minutes.
7. Serve hot with cream or ice cream. Makes 4 servings.

Clockwise from left: Hot Fruit Salad, Pear Dumpling, Whipped cream, Marzipan Peach

Marzipan Peaches

3/4 cup crumbled macaroons
Juice and grated peel of 1 orange
4 large firm peaches, halved, pitted
Cornstarch
12 oz. marzipan
1 egg white, slightly beaten
Sugar

To decorate:
4 small bay leaves
Whipped cream

---

1. Lightly grease a baking sheet. In a small bowl, combine macaroons and orange juice. Let stand 20 minutes.
2. Preheat oven to 375F (190C).
3. Divide macaroon mixture among 4 peach halves. Top with remaining halves.
4. Roll each filled peach lightly in cornstarch.
5. On a surface lightly dusted with cornstarch, roll out marzipan to 1/8-inch thick. Cut 4 (6-inch-diameter) circles.
6. Stand a filled peach in center of each marzipan circle. Pull up edges of marzipan to completely enclose peach. Seal edges.
7. Place marzipan-covered peaches on greased baking sheet. Brush with beaten egg white; sprinkle with sugar and orange peel.
8. Bake in preheated oven 15 minutes or until golden brown.
9. Decorate each peach with a bay leaf. Serve warm with whipped cream. Makes 4 servings.

Variation
If desired, roll glazed marzipan-covered peaches in sugar-and-orange-peel mixture rather than sprinkling with the mixture. Or, substitute chopped, blanched almonds for the sugar-and-orange-peel mixture.

This unusual recipe is worth the careful preparation and cooking required to ensure an attractive appearance. It will make an impressive finale to a dinner party.

Choose peaches that are ripe but still firm. If peaches are too soft, they will not hold their shape when cooked. The marzipan must be soft and pliable before starting to mold it around the filled peaches. Otherwise it will crack and not seal tightly around peaches. Glaze evenly with beaten egg white so that baked marzipan-covered peaches have an even golden crust.

Pear Dumplings

4 large pears, peeled
Juice of 1 lemon
Pastry for a double-crust pie
1 egg, beaten
1/4 cup orange marmalade

To serve:
Ice cream or whipped cream

---

1. Preheat oven to 375F (190C). Grease a baking sheet.
2. Carefully remove core from base of each pear, so that stem end of each pear is left intact. Brush prepared pears with lemon juice to prevent browning.
3. Divide pastry in half. On a lightly floured surface, roll out 1/2 of pastry into a 14 " x 7" rectangle. Repeat with remaining pastry.
4. Brush edges of pastry squares with beaten egg.
5. Fill base of each pear with 1 tablespoon marmalade.
6. Carefully place a filled pear in center of each pastry square. Pull up pastry edges around pear, pressing edges together at stem end. Cut off excess pastry; reserve for decorations.
7. Place pastry-covered pears on greased baking sheet; brush with egg to glaze.
8. If desired, roll out pastry trimmings; cut small leaves to decorate. Attach leaves; brush with egg.
9. Bake in preheated oven 35 minutes. Serve hot with ice cream or whipped cream. Makes 4 servings.

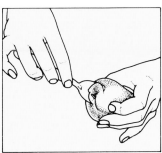 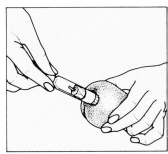

1/Carefully remove core from base of pear with a teaspoon.

2/Or, remove core from base of pear with an apple corer.

Family Treats

Party Lights

Ice Cubes:
Green food coloring
Maraschino cherries

Lemonade:
1/3 cup lemon juice
3/4 cup sugar
1 qt. water (4 cups)
Yellow food coloring, if desired

Kids love bright colors, especially in drinks. Brightly colored drinks can be made with very little effort. For an extra touch, add contrasting colored ice cubes.

1. To make green ice cubes, measure capacity of ice-cube tray by filling it with water. Pour water into a measuring cup.
2. Add enough green food coloring to water to give desired color.
3. Place a maraschino cherry in each ice-cube compartment; pour in green water. Freeze until solid.
4. In a pitcher, combine ingredients for lemonade. Stir until sugar dissolves. Refrigerate until chilled.
5. Place 2 to 3 green ice cubes into each glass; fill with lemonade. Makes 4 servings.

Peanut Sandwich Balls

1 (8-oz.) pkg. cream cheese, room temperature
2 tablespoons peanut butter
1/2 cup finely chopped ham
3 tablespoons fresh bread crumbs
1/4 cup finely chopped peanuts

1. In a medium bowl, beat cream cheese and peanut butter with a wooden spoon until smooth.
2. Beat in ham and bread crumbs.
3. Shape mixture into about 24 small balls. Roll each ball in chopped peanuts until evenly coated.
4. Insert a wooden pick into each ball. Makes 24 balls.

Coconut Funny Faces

6 tablespoons butter or margarine, room temperature
1/3 cup sugar
3 egg yolks
1/2 teaspoon vanilla extract
1-1/4 cups sifted all-purpose flour
1 cup flaked or shredded coconut

To decorate:
6 to 8 tablespoons apple jelly or orange marmalade
1/4 cup flaked or shredded coconut
1 tablespoon unsweetened cocoa powder
12 red candied cherries
Assorted candies

These cookies are guaranteed to put a smile on anyone's face.

1. In a large bowl, beat butter or margarine and sugar until light and fluffy. Beat in egg yolks and vanilla until blended.
2. Fold in flour and coconut. Shape dough into a flattened ball; wrap in plastic wrap or foil. Refrigerate 30 minutes.
3. Preheat oven to 350F (175C). Grease 2 baking sheets. On a lightly floured surface, roll out chilled dough to 1/8 inch thickness. Cut dough into 24 rounds with a plain 2-1/2- inch cookie cutter. Place cookies on greased baking sheets.
4. Bake in preheated oven 12 to 15 minutes or until golden brown. Remove from baking sheets; cool on wire racks.
5. To decorate, spread jelly or marmalade over flat side of 1/2 of cookies; top with remaining cookies.
6. In a small bowl, toss coconut and cocoa powder together until coconut is blended.
7. Spread a little jelly or marmalade around top edge of each cookie sandwich; sprinkle with cocoa-coated coconut for hair.
8. Cut cherries in half; attach to cookies with a dab of jelly or marmalade for eyes. Make mouth and nose with small candies. Makes 12 cookies.

Clockwise from left: Party Lights, Coconut Funny Faces, Peanut Sandwich Balls

Left to right: Flying Saucers, Cheesy Twists, Marbled Eggs, Tub O'Beans

Flying Saucers

Pastry for a double-crust pie
1 cup chopped ham
1 cup shredded cheese (4 oz.)
3 tablespoons ketchup
Freshly ground pepper
1/2 cup chopped peanuts, if desired
1 egg, beaten

To garnish:
4 pickled onions
Thin cucumber slices
Pimentos, cut into leaf shapes

1. Preheat oven to 375F (190C). On a lightly floured surface, roll out pastry to 1/8 inch thick. Cut out 8 (5-inch) circles.
2. Line 4 (4-1/4-inch) tart pans with pastry.
3. In a medium bowl, combine ham, cheese, ketchup, pepper and peanuts, if desired.
4. Divide filling among pastry-lined pans. Brush pastry edges with beaten egg.
5. Lay remaining pastry circles over filling. Press edges together to seal. Glaze top surface of pastry with beaten egg. Place tarts on a baking sheet.
6. Bake in preheated oven 30 to 35 minutes or until pastry is golden brown.
7. Decorate as shown in photo with onions, cucumber and pimentos. Serve hot or cold. Makes 4 servings.

Cheesy Twists

4 oz. puff pastry, thawed, if frozen
1 egg, beaten
3/4 cup grated Parmesan cheese (2 oz.)
2 tablespoons sesame seeds

1. On a lightly floured board, roll out pastry to a 12-inch square.
2. Cut pastry into 2 equal rectangles.
3. Brush 1 pastry rectangle with beaten egg; sprinkle with cheese.
4. Top with second pastry rectangle. Roll lightly to press 2 pastry rectangles together.
5. Brush top surface of pastry lightly with beaten egg; sprinkle with sesame seeds.
6. Cut into 6 (6- x 1/2-inch) strips.
7. Twist each strip 2 or 3 times, bringing ends together to form a circle. Press ends to seal. Rinse a baking sheet with water. Place circles on damp baking sheet. Refrigerate 30 minutes.
8. Preheat oven to 425F (220C).
9. Bake in preheated oven 12 minutes or until golden brown. Makes 24 rings.

Marbled Eggs

6 eggs
About 2 teaspoons food coloring

These attractive mottled eggs are very simple to make. They add interest to a packed school lunch or picnic. Use your choice of colors.

1. Place eggs in a medium saucepan; add enough cold water to completely cover.
2. Bring water to a boil; simmer eggs 3 minutes. Remove eggs carefully with a slotted spoon.
3. Add enough food coloring to cooking water to tint it a deep color.
4. Tap eggs all over with back of a spoon to crack shells.
5. Return eggs to colored water; simmer 7 minutes.
6. Fill a medium bowl 1/2 full of iced water; add 2 teaspoons additional food coloring. Place eggs in iced water.
7. When cool, peel eggs. Makes 6 hard-cooked eggs.

Tub O'Beans

8 individual round whole-wheat-bread loaves
Vegetable oil
1 (15-oz.) can baked beans
1 (11-oz.) can whole-kernel corn, drained
4 large frankfurters, chopped

1. Preheat oven to 375F (190C). Cut a thin slice from top of each loaf. Carefully hollow out centers, leaving shells about 1/2 inch thick. Use centers for bread crumbs, if desired.
2. Brush inside of hollowed loaves with oil.
3. Place loaves on a baking sheet. Bake in preheated oven 10 minutes or until loaves are crisp.
4. Meanwhile, in a medium saucepan, combine beans, corn and frankfurters. Stir over medium heat until hot.
5. Divide bean mixture among baked loaves; wrap each filled loaf in foil.
6. Bake 10 minutes.
7. Remove foil; serve warm. Makes 8 servings.

Banana Pops

6 large firm bananas, peeled
12 wooden skewers or wooden ice-cream sticks
12 oz. semisweet or milk chocolate

To decorate:
Colored shot or chocolate sprinkles
Frosting
Candied fruit

The banana with a difference! Let children decorate their own Banana Pops. Some suggestions are a child's name piped in icing, a face made from small colored candies, or numbers to celebrate a birthday.

1. Cut each banana in half crosswise.
2. Insert a wooden skewer or stick at least 2 inches inside each banana half.
3. Place skewered bananas on a piece of foil. Freeze 1 hour or until firm.
4. Break chocolate into pieces. Place chocolate pieces in the top of a double boiler over simmering water. Stir until chocolate melts.
5. Taking 1 banana from freezer at a time, hold it over chocolate. Spoon melted chocolate over banana until evenly coated. If bananas are frozen, chocolate coating will start to set immediately.
6. As soon as each banana is coated with chocolate, sprinkle with colored shot, chocolate sprinkles or any decoration of your choice.
7. When each banana has been coated with chocolate and decorated, lay it carefully on a sheet of lightly oiled waxed paper. Or, push wooden handles into a large block of florist foam.
8. As soon as chocolate coating has set on bananas and decorations are firmly in place, wrap banana pops lightly in foil or freezer wrap. Return to freezer. Serve without thawing. Makes 12 servings.

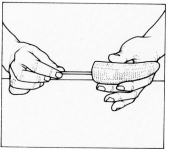

1/Insert a wooden skewer or stick at least 2 inches inside each banana half.

2/Spoon melted chocolate over banana until evenly coated.

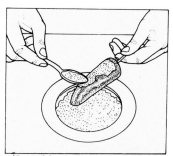

3/Sprinkle with colored shot, chocolate sprinkles or any decoration of your choice.

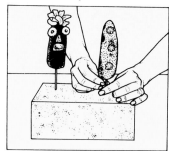

4/Push wooden handles into a large block of florist foam.

Banana Pops

Orange-Banana Floats

5 small bananas, peeled
Juice of 1 lemon
2 tablespoons honey
1 qt. orange juice (4 cups)
Ice cubes
6 scoops vanilla ice cream
6 thin orange slices, if desired

This makes a delicious party drink for kids. Serve it with spoons so that none of the ice cream is wasted at the bottom of the glass.

1. Chop bananas. In a blender or food processor fitted with a steel blade, process chopped bananas, lemon juice and honey until smooth.
2. Add 1/2 of orange juice; process until blended.
3. Pour orange-and-banana mixture into a large pitcher; stir in remaining orange juice. Add a few ice cubes.
4. Place a scoop of ice cream into each of 6 tall tumblers. Pour over orange-and-banana mixture.
5. Make a small cut in each orange slice; place over rim of each glass, if desired. Serve immediately with straws and long-handled spoons. Makes 6 servings.

Animal Sandwiches

6 whole-wheat-bread slices
Butter or margarine, room temperature
2 (4-1/2-oz.) cans deviled ham
2 small pkgs. potato chips

If you use small animal-cookie cutters, you should be able to get 4 open sandwiches from each slice of bread. If you don't have animal shapes, use any other decorative cookie cutters.

1. Spread slices of bread with butter or margarine; then spread with a thin layer of deviled ham.
2. Crush potato chips with a rolling pin. Press crushed chips onto ham-covered bread slices.
3. Cut animal shapes from potato chip-topped bread, using animal-cookie cutters. Makes 18 to 24 small sandwiches depending on size of cutter.

Butterfly-Wing Cookies

3 egg yolks
1/2 cup sugar
1/2 cup half and half
2 teaspoons vanilla extract
2-2/3 cups all-purpose flour
Vegetable oil for deep-fat frying
Powdered sugar, if desired

1. In a large bowl, beat egg yolks, sugar, half and half and vanilla until blended.
2. Stir in flour to make a smooth dough.
3. On a lightly floured surface, roll out dough to a 16" x 10" rectangle. Cut out 24 diamond shapes with a fluted pastry wheel.
4. Cut a small slit in center of each diamond. Tuck opposite points of diamond through slit and pull through slightly, as shown below.
5. Heat oil in a deep-fryer or saucepan to 375F (190C) or until a 1-inch bread cube turns golden brown in 50 seconds. Carefully place 4 to 6 cookies into hot oil. Deep-fry 3 to 4 minutes or until golden and crisp.
6. Remove deep-fried cookies with a slotted spoon; drain on paper towels. Repeat with remaining cookies. Sprinkle with sifted powdered sugar, if desired. Makes 24 cookies.

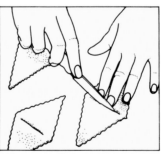
1/Cut a small slit in center of each diamond.

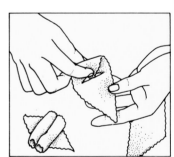
2/Tuck opposite points of diamond through slit and pull through slightly.

Clockwise from left: Butterfly-Wing Cookies, Orange-Banana Floats, Animal Sandwiches

Orange-Cup Trifles

8 large navel oranges
1 (3-oz.) pkg. orange-flavored gelatin
4 pound-cake or sponge-cake slices
1 (16-oz.) can sliced peaches or pears, drained
1-1/2 cups sweetened whipped cream

To decorate:
Candied orange slices
Candied lemon slices

These orange cups can be filled the day before you plan to serve them. Decorate with whipped cream just before serving. Use large oranges, if available.

1. Cut a thick slice from stem end of each orange; discard slices.
2. Carefully hollow out oranges with a grapefruit spoon. Remove seeds, membrane and white pith from orange pulp. Chop pulp, reserving juice. Measure juice; add enough water to make 1 cup. Pour juice mixture into a small saucepan; bring to a boil.
3. Place orange gelatin in a medium bowl; pour in hot orange-juice mixture. Stir until gelatin is completely dissolved. Stir in 1 cup cold water. Refrigerate until gelatin is thick and syrupy.
4. Cut cake slices and peaches or pears into small cubes. In a medium bowl, combine cake cubes, peach or pear cubes and chopped oranges. Spoon mixture evenly into orange shells; pack down lightly. Spoon orange gelatin over filled oranges. Refrigerate until gelatin is completely set, about 3 hours.
5. Pipe or spoon whipped cream decoratively on top of orange cups. Decorate with candied orange and lemon slices. Makes 8 servings.

Coffee Shortbread Cookies

1/2 cup finely ground almonds
1-1/4 cups all-purpose flour, sifted
3/4 cup powdered sugar
2 tablespoons instant coffee powder
3/4 cup butter or margarine, room temperature
Granulated sugar

---

1. In a large bowl, combine almonds, flour, powdered sugar and coffee until blended. Add butter or margarine; beat at medium speed until blended, scraping down side of bowl occasionally.
2. Shape dough into a ball. Wrap in plastic wrap or foil; refrigerate 30 minutes.
3. Preheat oven to 350F (175C). On a lightly floured surface, roll out dough to about 1/4 inch thick. Cut dough with a 1-1/2- to 2-inch-floured plain or fluted cookie cutter.
4. Place cookies about 1 inch apart on ungreased baking sheets. Sprinkle with granulated sugar.
5. Bake 10 to 12 minutes or until edges are just firm. Remove from baking sheets; cool on wire racks. Makes 60 to 66 cookies.

Chocolate Refrigerator Bars

1/2 cup butter or margarine
1/3 cup sugar
5 tablespoons unsweetened cocoa powder
1 egg, beaten
1 teaspoon vanilla extract
1 cup shredded or flaked coconut
1/3 cup chopped pecans
8 whole graham crackers, crushed

Butter Icing:
1/4 cup butter or margarine, room temperature
1-3/4 cups powdered sugar, sifted
1 egg

Chocolate Topping:
6 oz. semisweet chocolate
1 tablespoon butter, room temperature

---

1. Grease a 9-inch-square baking pan.
2. Melt butter or margarine and sugar in a small saucepan over low heat, stirring until smooth.
3. Stir in cocoa, egg and vanilla. Cook until mixture thickens, stirring constantly.
4. Remove from heat; stir in coconut, pecans and crushed crackers. Press mixture evenly into greased pan. Refrigerate 1 hour.
5. To make Butter Icing, in a small bowl, beat butter or margarine, powdered sugar and egg until smooth and creamy. Spread over refrigerated chocolate mixture. Return to refrigerator until icing is firm.
6. To make Chocolate Topping, melt chocolate and butter in a small heavy saucepan over low heat, stirring until smooth. Swirl chocolate over icing. Refrigerate 3 to 4 hours. Cut into squares. Makes 16 to 20 squares.

Carrot Cookies

1/2 cup butter or margarine, room temperature
1/2 cup sugar
1 egg
1/4 cup orange marmalade
1-1/2 cups grated carrots (about 2 medium carrots)
1-1/3 cups all-purpose flour
1/2 teaspoon salt
1/2 teaspoon baking powder
1/2 cup chopped raisins

1. Preheat oven to 350F (175C). Lightly grease 2 baking sheets.
2. In a medium bowl, beat butter or margarine and sugar until light and fluffy. Beat in egg until blended. Stir in marmalade and carrots.
3. Sift flour, salt and baking powder over butter mixture. Fold in dry ingredients and raisins. Drop rounded teaspoons of mixture, about 1-1/2 inches apart, on greased baking sheets.
4. Bake in preheated oven 12 to 15 minutes or until golden around edges. Remove from baking sheets; cool on wire racks. Makes about 48 cookies.

Left to right: Orange-Cup Trifles, Chocolate Refrigerator Bars

Orange & Walnut Fondant

1 lb. powdered sugar, sifted
1 egg white, slightly beaten
2 to 3 tablespoons whipping cream
Finely grated peel of 1 orange
Orange food coloring
Powdered sugar
1 cup finely chopped walnuts (4 oz.)

To decorate:
Walnut halves

This is a recipe for uncooked fondant. Whether you're experienced at candymaking or a novice, this is the recipe for you!

1. In a medium bowl, combine 1 lb. powdered sugar, egg white, 2 tablespoons whipping cream and orange peel. Add additional whipping cream, if necessary to make a firm paste.
2. On a surface lightly coated with powdered sugar, knead until smooth. Knead in enough food coloring to tint a pale orange; add 1 drop at a time. Knead until blended.
3. Knead chopped walnuts into fondant.
4. Dust your hands with powdered sugar. Shape fondant into cherry-size balls. Press into oval shapes.
5. Place shaped fondants on a wire rack; press a walnut half into top of each 1.
6. Let dry 8 hours or overnight. Store tightly covered. Makes about 1-1/4 pounds.

Top to bottom: Sherried Prunes, Chocolate Bon Bons, Orange & Walnut Fondant

Sherried Prunes

2 lb. large prunes
1 (3-inch strip) lemon peel
2 bay leaves
Medium-dry sherry

It is difficult to give an exact quantity of sherry, as the amount of sherry absorbed will vary. Prepare 2 to 3 months in advance. These make excellent gifts.

1. Place prunes in a 1-1/2-qt. jar with a lid. Add lemon peel and bay leaves.
2. Add enough sherry to cover prunes. Seal tightly; let stand in a cool place 1 week.
3. Add additional sherry to replace what has been absorbed.
4. Continue adding additional sherry every week for 2 months. Makes 1-1/2 quarts.

Spiced Apple Butter

4 lb. cooking apples, cut into small pieces
Grated peel of 1 lemon
1/2 teaspoon ground cinnamon
1/2 teaspoon ground ginger
1/2 teaspoon ground mace
Water
2 cups sugar

1. In a large saucepan, combine apples, lemon peel and spices. Add enough water to half cover apples. Simmer gently until apples are soft.
2. Press apples and liquid through a sieve.
3. Place apple puree in a clean, large saucepan. Stir in sugar.
4. Stir over low heat until sugar dissolves. Simmer until thick and creamy, stirring frequently.
5. Ladle hot apple butter into hot, clean 1/2-pint or 1-pint canning jars, leaving 1/4-inch headspace. Seal with canning lids, following manufacturer's directions.
6. Place filled jars in canner. Process jars in a boiling-water bath 10 minutes. Makes about 2 pints.

To process jars in a boiling water bath, place filled and sealed jars in canner. Cover jars with 1 to 2 inches hot, not boiling, water. Cover canner; bring water to a full boil. Begin counting processing time. Reduce heat until water boils gently. Process for time given in recipe.

Chocolate Bon Bons

20 maraschino cherries
1 (8-oz.) pkg. marzipan
8 oz. semisweet chocolate, melted

These small chocolate-and-marzipan-covered cherries make a wonderful gift for anyone with a sweet tooth.

1. Lightly oil a large sheet of waxed paper; set aside. Lay maraschino cherries on paper towels to absorb excess maraschino syrup.
2. Divide marzipan into 20 equal pieces; knead each until smooth.
3. Carefully mold each marzipan piece around a cherry, making sure that cherries are completely enclosed.
4. Dip each marzipan-covered cherry into melted chocolate with a fork. Place cherries on a piece of lightly oiled waxed paper; leave until set.
5. Place a little melted chocolate into a small pastry bag fitted with a writing tip; pipe a chocolate swirl on top of each bon bon. Leave until set. Makes 20 bon bons.

Peanut-Butter Crispies

1 (12-oz.) pkg. milk chocolate pieces
1 cup smooth or crunchy peanut butter
2 cups crisp rice cereal
1 cup chopped nuts
1 teaspoon vanilla

1. Grease an 11" x 7" pan.
2. In a heavy, medium saucepan combine chocolate pieces and peanut butter. Stir over low heat until chocolate melts and mixture is smooth.
3. Remove from heat; stir in vanilla. In a large bowl, combine cereal and nuts. Pour chocolate mixture over cereal mixture. Stir until coated. Press mixture into greased pan.
4. Refrigerate until firm. Cut into squares. Makes about 35 squares.

Index